Make Your Own

BEER

A GUIDE TO ALL THINGS BEER & HOW TO BREW IT YOURSELF

JOHN SHEPHERD

Make Your Own BEER

A GUIDE TO ALL THINGS BEER & HOW TO BREW IT YOURSELF

JOHN SHEPHERD

WHITE OWL

First published in Great Britain in 2020 by
Pen & Sword WHITE OWL
An imprint of
Pen & Sword Books Ltd
Yorkshire – Philadelphia

ISBN 9781526769978

Printed and bound in India by Replika Press Pvt. Ltd.

Pen & Sword Books Limited incorporates the imprints of Atlas, Archaeology, Aviation, Discovery, Family History, Fiction, History, Maritime, Military, Military Classics, Politics, Select, Transport, True Crime, Air World, Frontline Publishing, Leo Cooper, Remember When, Seaforth Publishing, The Praetorian Press, Wharncliffe Local History, Wharncliffe Transport, Wharncliffe True Crime and White Owl.

For a complete list of Pen & Sword titles please contact

PEN & SWORD BOOKS LIMITED
47 Church Street, Barnsley, South Yorkshire, S70 2AS, England
E-mail: enquiries@pen-and-sword.co.uk
Website: www.pen-and-sword.co.uk

Or
PEN AND SWORD BOOKS
1950 Lawrence Rd, Havertown, PA 19083, USA
E-mail: Uspen-and-sword@casematepublishers.com
Website: www.penandswordbooks.com

Contents

The Truman Brewery in London, an institution.

(© Hamish/Adobe Stock)

Chapter One

The History of Beer

BEER HAS BEEN a part of life for hundreds, more likely thousands, of years, with traces of a beer-type substance found on 5,000-year-old Chinese pottery. Ignoring the question over what defines a 'beer-type substance' and what that actually means for the history of beer, that is a long time. Beer's role has changed many times over that period and, as well as being enjoyed, it has also played a vital function as an essential part of the human diet. The brewing process meant that it was a safer product to consume than many sources of water, even though those producing and consuming it may not have realised how or why it came to have these benefits. This may explain the numerous tales of many people, for example workers during the Industrial Revolution, drinking beer at all hours of the day in the same way that water is consumed today. As well as not containing some of the elements that made unclean water dangerous, some would argue that beer has some health benefits, if drunk sensibly, but that argument can continue elsewhere. The focus of this book is how to produce beer, though some historical context never did any harm.

As with many other products that have been around for a long period, from its humble origins, beer came to be an important commercial commodity. Within a capitalist society that often means commercial pressures can lead to variations in what is produced and how it is consumed. The free market can only go so far; products created are normally a combination of public demand and the business sector's desire to supply it. This is especially true in the UK, where the eventual structure of the pub and beer industry was not just left to the free market but became a combination of legislation and economic priorities, as well as public demand.

In the UK in the nineteenth century, commercial brewers came to be very powerful and important organisations, and initially the beer they produced was regional and centred as much on practicality as taste. The famous Trent brewing industry was based on the characteristics of the natural water supply and possibly the nearby presence of lots of thirsty workers. In other areas, the styles of beer also tended to complement the type and availability of raw materials. There are also examples of regional breweries being family owned and firmly invested in their communities. So the beers tended to reflect the region and the wealthy benefactors that the industry created and this meant the breweries were strongly entwined in local infrastructure. It was not only about the products but just as much about the institution that produced it and the regions in which they existed. This is not to suggest that it was some sort of capitalist utopia, with

Welcome to the classic British pub.
(© pawopa3336/Adobe Stock)

industry, worker and consumer all in perfect harmony, far from it. However it is reasonable to conclude that before logistics were revolutionised and long before globalisation happened, brewing was a relatively regional business that invested, in one form or another, in its community.

The history of the pub in the UK is also a unique market, since there has always been a strong link between those producing the beer and those selling it (with pubs historically being the main source of supply). Again, a lot more has been written and argued on this point elsewhere, but tied houses, whereby the pubs were owned or controlled by the brewery, became more and more prevalent. Not surprisingly, as the business people (and ultimately the shareholders) running and owning the breweries became more commercial, so financial pressures became more important. This culminated in the situation in the second half of the twentieth century where breweries began to consolidate and many regional breweries were swallowed up by big, growing, national breweries. The control they exerted over both production and supply meant that these new mega-breweries could dictate the products that reached the consumer and, for commercial reasons, this often meant profit ruled over quality and taste. When the same business controls what is made and where it is sold, it is not surprising that the choice for the consumer becomes limited.

If in need of a debating topic down the pub, consider whether the US-led craft beer revolution (where ownership and supply is more fragmented and segmented) would have happened in quite the same way within the UK's 'restricted' free market. Incidentally, having worked within the commercial sector for a number of years and having spent a lot of time trying to sell independent craft beer into pubs and pub chains, be under no illusion about the freedom of the pub sector. It may not be quite as closed a shop as it used to be but it is still very difficult for a small and/or new entrant to gain effective access. The power of the 'pubco' may have been reduced, but only in the way a highly powered car might obey the speed limit, however only if someone is watching.

It is reasonable to conclude that this restricted market situation is a significant part of what led to the decline of the UK's traditional beer style, cask ales, at the expense of keg-based substitutes. A whole book could be written on the cask versus the keg but a key point of difference is the secondary fermentation and this is looked at in more detail in Chapter 3. For now, what is important is that the keg beers were cheaper to produce (partly because of savings associated with the mass production of generic/similar beer styles) and because they had a longer product life it meant pubs could keep the beer for longer. An additional benefit, for the producers, of this approach is that it also required less input and skill on the part of the publican. This led to a whole generation of standardised

Different styles, different beers, different tastes.
(© Rido/Adobe Stock)

Empty casks, beer poured, awaiting collection.
(© Imran's Photography/Adobe Stock)

beers being produced in the UK and it was a reaction to this and the decline of the cask- conditioned beers that led directly to the formation of CAMRA in 1971.

If the pub discussion that was proposed earlier is still going on, consider something even more contentious (as it may be harder to find evidence to back this up): were the pubcos effectively shooting themselves in the foot in the long term by creating a product without any unique or better quality attributes? Think about the products a pub sells and it is only cask-conditioned beer that cannot be easily replicated at home or in the retail environment. Wine, spirits and lagers are all products that can be sold by a supermarket and consumed at home. However, cask-conditioned beer, despite the best innovative efforts, can only really be

A traditional cask racked up and ready. (© John Shepherd)

A keg with valve and hoses connected, ready to pour. (© John Shepherd)

sold from a pub. So, by effectively ringing in the changes and making cask beer redundant, were the pubs communicating the message to customers that they no longer needed the skill of the publican to supply the beer: that they could focus instead on the convenience of the supermarket? This is a good pub discussion because it cannot be properly concluded; cask-conditioned beer did not become extinct and CAMRA has to take some credit for that.

CAMRA (the Campaign For Real Ale) was at the forefront of promoting the quality benefits of cask ale over the keg ales of the time and their influence has grown considerably over the forty-plus years that they have been campaigning. However, while they did a lot for cask ales, many would argue that they are not the only reason for the recent resurgence in variety and quality. Those same people might argue that CAMRA's ongoing focus on cask-conditioned rather than variety and quality may even now be damaging its reputation. It seems to be painting itself into a bit of a corner, whereby anything that is not cask-conditioned is deemed inferior. CAMRA were certainly essential – fighting the good fight when very few others were – but it could be said that the real role model for the current move towards craft beer style products originated in the most unlikely of places. In the UK, the battle lines had been drawn between the packaging and delivery method: that is cask versus keg. But elsewhere the fight

What a poured cask-conditioned beer should look like. (© F-Stop Boy/Adobe Stock)

What American craft brewers sometimes look like.
(© Fxquadro/ Adobe Stock)

was over the quality and taste of the beer rather than what it was put into.

In North America in the late 1970s and early 1980s, craft brewers began to spring up in very humble surroundings with a mission to provide quality alternatives to the generic lager offering from most American brewers. They certainly took inspiration from classic UK beer styles, but they did a number of things differently: a focus on local, a focus on quality and a focus on taste. While this might sound a little like the original motivation for the British regional breweries, there is one fundamental difference: the US breweries were trying to do all of this in a keg format. Cask ale was (and largely still is) very rare in the US, for perhaps the same reason as it declined in the UK – commercial and practical priorities. But rather than fight against the packaging, the US brewers fought against the product that was being put into that packaging. This was helped by the availability of significantly different versions of the ingredients. So the hops that UK brewers had traditionally used were more about bittering than flavour and aroma, but American brewers used hop varieties that had much more natural flavour (and aroma) from areas such as the north-west, where the climate is much more vibrant (there is more discussion on hop varieties and qualities in Chapter 5). So it was that very traditional beers from the UK, such as IPAs, were given an American makeover and became the paler, lighter and even more flavoursome beers that are available today.

The revolution was led by small-scale brewers who seemed to be primarily based on the West Coast but were not restricted to that part of the US. One thing that made these innovators different from their big-business rivals, both in the UK and the US, was that they were enthusiastic consumers of the product as well as producers. When you read about the people that started these breweries, it is remarkable how so many of them say something along the lines of 'I just wanted a good beer' or 'We were not in it for the money' or 'It was all about the product, not the profit'. It is hard to believe that the shareholders of the big, global beer companies were even drinking their product, let alone savouring it. The American craft beer revolution took off and while it was still only a relatively small proportion of the total beer sales, the size of the North American market meant it was still a big business, it was growing rapidly and it had the thing that established corporations rarely have: momentum.

Back in the UK, real ale was starting to make a comeback and the growing demand for quality over profit, which had been a factor in the US craft sector, was beginning to impact the UK market. As well as the UK consumer becoming

Three classic American 'craft' beers. (© Philip Shepherd)

Two classic British 'craft' beers. (© Philip Shepherd)

more demanding at this time, there must have been some impact from the small, but growing, presence of US craft beers. For example, Sierra Nevada had become pretty much nationally available in the US in the mid-1990s and a few years later it was starting to be seen in the UK. This must have contributed something to the movement, over the past ten years, towards beer becoming fashionable again and many consumers being less obsessed with quantity and much more interested in quality. The number of breweries in the UK (including small craft breweries) is now back at the level it was at in the 1930s, before the consolidation took place. Things really have gone full circle, with these smaller breweries making the most of the quality of their beers, the use of the best ingredients and, like the original local breweries, making the most of their community connections. This is one area where the pubcos have relented somewhat, in that it is fairly common to go into a pub and see, alongside the national mass-produced beers, a local product. Whether this is done to support local breweries or as a compromise to choice without going too far is for the individual to decide (or go back to that pub discussion).

Looking back at the recent history of beer in the UK, the role of CAMRA in highlighting the plight of the cask ale was important, but the current UK craft beer market is not just about cask ale. It is about a quality product, whether cask or keg, bottle or can. As in the US experience, it has increasingly become about consumers wanting the goods but also the brewers having an interest in their product. The vast majority of the new, small craft breweries are run by people who love the beer that they are producing and are not just in it for the profit, just like their American counterparts that came before them.

Alongside the growth of craft brewing businesses, there has been a knock-on resurgence in the home-brew market, as beer lovers have begun to realise that the availability of ingredients and equipment means that they too can get involved. In the same way that industrial brewing led to inferior products, home brewing in the same period was all about convenience over quality. Malt extracts were everywhere, so rather than creating your own wort and beers from the raw materials, it was almost as basic as buying a couple of packs of pre-made ingredients, mixing together and let them ferment. Home-brewed beer, as a result, became the butt of many jokes. By going back to basics and focusing on recipes and ingredients, rather than a cheap and simple process, people have begun to appreciate that they too can brew their own great beers. This book is not going to look at, in any detail, the malt extract approach because it does not really require any explanation. If that is your preferred approach to home brewing that is fine but it does not really require a book about it.

This book will outline what you need to do in order to create your own great beers from scratch. It will contain some factual information and some established best practice but also be flavoured with a certain amount of personal opinion and suggestions. It is intended to be an introduction to the world of home brewing and to give you, the reader, enough understanding so that you can make your own decisions about how much time, effort and expense you want to devote to this hobby/pastime/passion. One recurring theme of the book is that it is possible to produce some excellent, high-quality beers at home without a massive investment in equipment and with relatively little experience. This book is intended to get anyone to that point – producing a great beer – and where it leads from there is very much up to the individual.

Enjoy.

A classic home-brew beer.
(© Philip Shepherd)

Chapter Two

An Introduction to Brewing and This Guide

The four basic ingredients: water, malt, hops and yeast. (© Philip Shepherd)

BREWING BEER IS a great thing to do. Brewing beer at home is even better. It is an interesting hobby that, normally, produces something great at the end. At its most basic it is quite a simple process, but another great thing about it is that a home brewer can go on to make it as intricate or keep it as simple as they wish. There are home brewers who have never brewed the same thing twice and there

are some who only ever brew the same thing. Although most keen home brewers have a spirit of adventure and want to try different things, it is not a requirement. Experimenting does make both the brewing and the drinking more interesting – if that is the chosen route – and the good news is that it is rare for it to end in disaster.

Which leads to another good thing about home brewing: it is a skill, and like any other skill, with practice and application it becomes easier and, as a result, a home brewer will rarely go too far wrong. The palette of basic ingredients (water, malt, hops and yeast) are fairly forgiving and although they and the brewer may occasionally produce beer that is a little below expectations, it will be perfectly fine to drink and then the process simply starts again.

It will be discussed in the next few chapters that the basics are relatively simple, and the brewer can expand in all manner of directions that brewing talents, equipment and ingredients allow. For this reason it does seem to be one of those skills that is relatively easy to pick up but quite difficult to master. It could be likened to skiing in that regard, which is something most people can do at a very basic level the first time, but to become an expert skier is very difficult, time-consuming and expensive. That seems to be a fairly accurate description of home brewing.

To speak personally, for a while, I have been home brewing for many years and in 2015, with an old friend, we decided to start a commercial craft brewery. To complement our home-brewing skills, we went on a commercial brewing course and then, quite simply, bought some commercial kit and started experimenting. We found it relatively easy to scale up our skills and our brews, and six months later we were selling commercially. Within our first twelve months of operation we won a Gold Award from SIBA (the Society of Independent Brewers) for our region of London and the South East, for a 3.9% Pale Ale. After a couple of years we expanded into keg beers and cans, which required a little more training and consultancy and things have grown from there, as well as picking up a fair number of regional and national awards along the way.

Three cask beers, ready for pouring. (© John Shepherd)

Two of our original cask beers, ready for sampling.
(© John Shepherd)

So, I do have experience of brewing in both a personal and professional environment, but for home brewing I tend to keep it simple. My home-brew kit is still very basic, as you will see throughout this book, and I would always prefer to focus more on the quality and variety of ingredients than the size and shininess of the equipment. With this in mind, I have taken that as a starting point for this book, which is not to say that anyone reading this book should do the same but that is the rationale behind the approach.

This book is aimed at beginners and, although there are suggestions and hints as to what a brewer with more skill and experience might wish to consider, the focus is on those new to brewing. The book's approach is to combine the theory with best practice and with a bit of experience. This seems an appropriate way to get a well-rounded perspective on how things work, what is effective and why other options might also be considered. There won't be too much sophistication on the process side and there will not be a rallying cry for lots of expenditure, because that is not what home brewing, for most people, is about. That is not to say spending lots of money on kit and creating some really complex recipes is to be discouraged – it is just not for everyone.

There will also be a deliberate attempt to keep it relatively light-hearted because, well, this is a 'How to...' book and while there is a requirement for clarity and seriousness, up to a point, the intention is for every reader to be enthused with the concept of home brewing. It will, inevitably, contain some purely personal thoughts, as well as recollection and understanding from one perspective, but the intention behind that is that it might give the reader something to think about.

So the approach of the book will be as follows: provide some information and context around the history of beer, the ingredients and equipment and get the reader considering what could be done. Then, step by step, it will go through the process of a brew, what needs to be done and what should be happening, and ultimately decide where to go next.

Because it is written as a book to be read, rather than a set of instructions, it is probably better to read it and take notes in order to follow the content and produce a simpler version that you could refer to while brewing. There are some appendices, for reference and guidance on the brew day itself, that will provide some other information and there will be regular references to check things online. There are some remarkable, and free, resources online, which will make the learning journey and brewing life that much easier, and these will be signposted as and when appropriate.

I hope you enjoy reading this guide and the journey that it should take you on. Enjoy the brewing, enjoy the drinking and stick with the cleaning.

Two of our beers, ready for photographing. © John Shepherd)

One of your beers? This could be you. © John Shepherd)

Chapter Three

What Can Be Achieved as a Home Brewer?

AS THE PROUD owner of this book, whether self-bought or received as a gift, it is probably reasonable to assume a level of familiarity with a good variety of beers. But that does not automatically mean an awareness of how different styles of beers are produced and packaged and this has direct implications for the home brewer. This chapter will undertake an introductory comparison of current commercial brewing (largely at a craft level) with home brewing and explain where there are similarities and where there are differences.

Historically, the prevalent type of beer in the UK was cask. As discussed in Chapter 1, cask-conditioned beer did decline for a number of reasons, one of which was that it does require careful handling and has a limited shelf life for a publican. This is because it goes through secondary fermentation in its packaging and the beer 'conditions' or ages, after being opened.

Cask beer therefore requires fermentation to occur under the direct influence

A cask beer racked-up and settling (before being opened. (© John Shepherd)

of the brewer in the (open) fermenting vessel; it is then packaged with enough life in the yeast for it to go through a secondary ferment in the cask. This secondary fermentation produces some additional alcohol but also the required levels of carbonation. Upon being opened, as the air comes into contact with the beer, it gradually conditions over a period of time. So, if a standard ale was opened on day one, it would condition over the course of a few days, reach its flavour and appearance peak perhaps two or three days in and by day four or five be on a gradual decline. So, it is a living, natural product that requires careful handling which, if done well, provides an excellent product. If not done well, it can leave a bad taste in the mouth (pun absolutely intended).

Cask-conditioned beer is a great example of risk and reward. There is the danger that if the beer is not handled correctly things go wrong, but the flip side of that is that if things go right it produces a product that most beer drinkers consider to be superior to any other form. Certainly most ale drinkers would claim that to be true.

The other two key beer types produced commercially are keg beers and lagers. Up to fermentation, keg beers tend to go through a relatively similar process to cask beers in production (certainly within a craft beer environment). Thereafter things are quite different as keg beers tend to be fermented, stored and conditioned in sealed vessels, so the carbonation created during primary

Poured cask beer at various stages of conditioning.
© Philip Shepherd)

What Can Be Achieved as a Home Brewer? *21*

Beers (before kegging) in sealed conditioning tanks. (© John Shepherd)

Beers being chilled in sealed tanks. (© John Shepherd)

A sealed tank at a constant pressure of CO2. (© John Shepherd)

Commercial craft brewers with possible malt profiles.
(© Philip Shepherd)

fermentation is kept within the beer. The packaging is also carried out within a sealed environment, so there is no air in contact with the beer at any point after the brewing process. There is normally some sort of filtering process because brewers do not want yeast left in suspension in the beer because they want to minimise secondary fermentation in the keg. Even when dispensed, as beer is removed from the keg, the space it vacates is filled, normally with CO_2 (carbon dioxide) or nitrogen, or a mix of the two, and so the beer remains in an air-free state and therefore does not condition or age at anything like the same rate, and lasts longer. This is clearly an advantage for a business owner, who does not have to spend time looking after the beer, does not need to know anything about conditioning and who will not have to throw cask-conditioned beer away if it is not consumed in a few days.

Lagers are packaged in a similar way to keg beers but they should be fermented and conditioned over a much longer period of time. Lager in German means a storehouse and this is from the period when the beer was brewed and left to ferment and condition over a significant part of the year, normally winter. Commercial brewers may have reduced this time period but perfect storage and precise temperature control are essential for a quality lager to be produced.

Because the production process for keg beer and lager is more technical and requires greater precision and more equipment and oversight, cask-style brewing will be the starting point for the home brewer. But although the process is based on cask beer production, the modern home brewer can create recipes and styles of beer that are far from traditional and much closer to keg beers, if they so choose. This is possible because most home brewers will package into bottles and so they can produce a type of hybrid beer: brewed like a cask beer and packaged unfiltered (so will go through secondary conditioning) but subsequent storage and consumption (carbonated and cold) can make it more like a keg beer.

If new to home brewing, as with many new skills, the best advice is to start

The essential ingredients, chosen for the brew.
(© Philip Shepherd)

simple, in terms of recipe creation and style of beer. Produce a somewhat forgiving ale, maybe a best bitter or a simple pale ale, which has a relatively simple malt profile, basic hop recipe and stable yeast. Then, as skills develop and understanding improves, start to use bolder ingredients and create more sophisticated beers, such as bold, hoppy, American IPAs or rich and complex stouts. Unless specifically looking to invest a lot of money in equipment (as discussed further in Chapter 4), the average home brewer will probably be limited to producing hybrid beers. However, this hybrid approach can allow for a lot of different and very good beers. Lagers would be a challenge for most home brewers but even some commercial craft brewers create pale ales with lager hops and call it a lager-style, so there is a lot that can be done. There will be more explanation of this in Chapter 5, when discussing ingredients and recipes.

In summary, most home brewers, cannot match everything a commercial brewer can achieve and it the process will probably require more time and effort at home because of the kit and volume disadvantages. But there is always a way to create something, even if it is based on creativity rather than sticking to the recipe. So, armed with the right ingredients and some dedication, a home brewer will be able to produce some excellent beers – and the great thing is that they will be creating exactly the type of beer that they choose.

Chapter Four
Equipment

THE AVAILABILITY OF ingredients for the home brewer (which is looked at in the next chapter) has increased significantly but equipment has also seen a vast improvement in terms of variety, quality and, as a result, price. It is a far, far cry from the plastic buckets and malt extract (not forgetting the large glass bottles with the plastic cork stoppers) from the High Street retailers of old.

Before getting too excited about what could be bought, it is important to consider the basics. There is no doubt that more expensive and sophisticated

An example of a standard and simple home-brew kit.
(© Philip Shepherd)

equipment will allow greater flexibility and precision in the brewing, but it is not essential. If just starting out, the basic home-brew equipment, as outlined below, is more than sufficient. Yes, there are limitations on certain things such as temperature control (both high and low) but there are ways around this. The most significant thing about basic equipment as a beginner is that everything is a little more hands-on and things might take slightly longer. For example, cooling the wort (post-boil) can still be done with basic kit, it just takes more time and more work. So, it is hard to argue against starting with the basic kit and then adding things as and when experience grows and there is a better understanding of where the most benefit can be gained for the money spent.

The basic, beginner's home-brew kit will normally consist of something like the following:

Copper/Kettle

This is normally a glorified, plastic tea urn with a simple temperature control (and thermostat) and usually with one electric element. The modification is a brewery-standard tap that allows for easy dispensing and it generally has a mesh filter that goes over the internal tap opening to minimise hop detritus coming through. This style of copper/kettle works perfectly well; it gets to the boil relatively quickly, but there is one significant drawback: it often lacks the precision to maintain a rolling boil without some manual tweaking of the temperature control (see Chapter 8).

The standard home-brew copper/kettle. (© Philip Shepherd)

The copper/kettle element and mesh filter. (© Philip Shepherd)

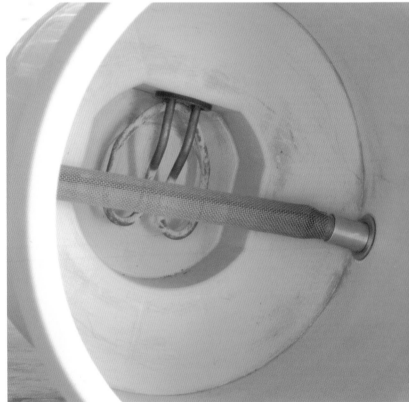

The mash tun in all its glory with hop filter. (© Philip Shepherd)

Mash tun

Another modified piece of kit, normally based on a small food or drink cooler (utilising the insulation) and with another brewery-standard tap. It normally comes with a simple, circular metal filter to reduce the amount of malt sediment that comes out during the sparge. Again, perfectly adequate and will actually do quite a good job of maintaining the mash temperature – one of the key requirements of this piece of kit.

Fermenting vessel (FV) buckets

These are pretty standard and can be purchased from any home-brew shop. They are normally between just over 20 litres and 25 litres and so are perfect for the

Home-brew FV vessel, with tap for decanting.
(© Philip Shepherd)

The regular home-brew FV, used for a number of purposes. (© Philip Shepherd)

normal sort of batch size for the home brewer. It's definitely useful to have two of these, as a minimum, and ideally one would have a tap on the front for easy bottling. It can make life easier for the home brewer, to use one during the brew, as an instant steriliser, and so consider having three as an easy option.

Cooling coil

This small, basic cooling coil, like its more sophisticated larger cousin, has a simple in and out for cooling fluid. The significant difference is that commercial cooling coils, normally an integral part of the structure of the vessels in a brewery, will

The home brewer's basic cooling coil. (© Philip Shepherd)

A commercial brewer's heat exchanger. (© John Shepherd)

connect to some sort of equipment so that the circulating fluid is constantly being cooled down, then heated as it runs through the coil and then cooled again. For the home-brew version, it is just one end onto the tap and one end down the sink. This is why if the ambient temperature is warm, then the groundwater from the tap will be warmer and the cooling will take longer.

Bottling equipment

At the most basic level, for bottling, a home brewer needs something with which to decant the fermented beer into another vessel (to get it off the yeast), a very

The bottling equipment for the end of the process. (© Philip Shepherd)

A slightly upgraded, but very useful, bottle capper.
(© Philip Shepherd)

basic bottling pipe to connect to that vessel and then some way of capping the bottles when filled. Multi-bottle fillers (where the filling is all done by gravity and balance and the bottles are just placed on the fillers) are a good time saver and also more accurate. But for the initial small quantities that will need bottling this is probably not worth it. It is worth buying a capper like the one pictured, as they are relatively cheap, don't normally come with the brew kit and are far and away the best option.

A quick note on the decanting hose to get the beer from the fermenting bucket, taking it off the yeast, and into the 'bottling bucket': the hose and filter arrangement used by most home brewers looks very basic and it is, but it does a great job. It is cheap, simple and perfectly adequate. If and when more technical and ambitious beers are attempted, this piece of kit may not do the job, but it is fine initially.

The all-important thermometer and hydrometer. (© Philip Shepherd)

The hydrometer in action, measuring the beer. (© Philip Shepherd)

Measuring

For all levels of brewing, the measuring of temperatures and gravities is key and the basic kit will do it, but this is one example where much better kit can be obtained by spending a relatively small amount of money. The thermometer and hydrometer (used for measuring gravity) normally available in home-brew shops tend to be quite small and so the calibration is quite limited, which reduces the accuracy. A special, calibrated, sample tube, which is tall and narrow for the thermometer and hydrometer to go into, is also required.

In this case, it does make sense to spend a bit more money on more professional

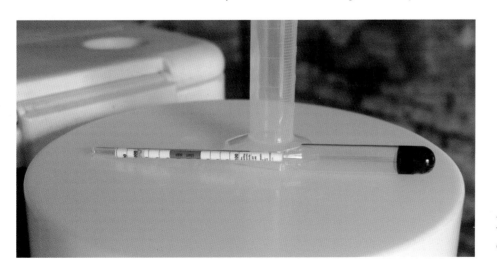

A slightly larger hydrometer than normal, making life easier. (© Philip Shepherd)

standard versions that are significantly larger and thus much more precise when taking readings. If going down that route, be aware that larger sample tubes will also be needed and it may require two hydrometers to cover the higher and the lower gravity readings. Definitely worth considering.

Sundry items

Look to source a few plastic or Pyrex measuring jugs, at least one of each, and they should really be at least a litre in volume. Buy decent plastic spoons for stirring etc. and potentially some hoses for decanting. A good set of digital scales will make life easier for measuring ingredients, but a regular kitchen set is fine.

Although it is not, strictly speaking, equipment, the environment or space within which the brewing will happen is also relevant to consider. The kitchen is clearly appropriate because of sinks and water access but be aware that the brewing will need quite a bit of space and the brew day will produce quite a lot of mess and a fair amount of smell. Some people are happy with the smell – which mainly comes during the boil – some people (normally the people not doing the brewing) are not. It is worth considering whether to sacrifice the sink and tap access in order to get out of the kitchen and avoid getting in the way. A decent-size garage or shed may well be a better bet. If not, wait for a weekend when the house is empty but, be warned, there will still be some lingering smells produced. If choosing to brew in the garage (or similar), just deal with the walk to the house for taps and sink and still do all the cleaning of equipment indoors, but have a fermenting bucket of water and peracetic for instant sterilising to hand.

Hopefully, that has given some insight into the equipment for a beginner to home brewing. If buying the standard decent kits then the big-ticket items (copper, mash tun, coils etc.) will be included and the other items will need to be sourced separately. A home-brew shop or website gives a lot of information on products needed and the options available, so that is often a good start. At the risk of being repetitive, most of the basic kit is fine to start with and then add other, more sophisticated kit over time. Basic kit can produce a great beer and expensive, state of the art kit can produce an average beer. It will often come down to who is doing the brewing and selecting the right ingredients, which is discussed in detail in the next chapter.

What all this equipment should end up producing.
(© Philip Shepherd)

Chapter Five
The Ingredients

AS COVERED IN the previous chapter, whereas with equipment there is normally a way to do something no matter what you're working with, when it comes to the ingredients you use, there is nowhere to hide. In the same way as making a great dish of food is dependent upon what is put in it, not the equipment that is used to cook it, so a great beer will rely upon great ingredients. Of course, kitchen and brewing equipment suppliers may disagree with this statement but if you only have a limited amount of time and or budget, then focus both on getting the ingredients right. With the growth of craft brewing and home

The quality ingredients that could and should be sourced and used. (© Philip Shepherd)

Your friendly, neighbourhood craft brewer. (© rh2010/Adobe Stock)

brewing, there are all sorts of recipes out there using the best ingredients – and the good news is that they're much more readily available than they used to be.

The home brewing revolution, following hard on the heels of the US-led craft beer revolution, has seen a lot of home brewers wanting the best possible ingredients in order to produce the best possible beers. Of course, the malt extract kits still exist and, to the unwary, appear to offer a great way into home brewing but it seems logical that the way to go is to use great, authentic, individual ingredients. By all means, simple 'add water' kits are a good gift for the difficult-to-buy-for uncle and they may well offer an introduction to brewing, but nothing can substitute for the real, good stuff.

The source of these ingredients can be a good home-brew shop or from the various online options that these days offer a great selection of the key ingredients: malt, hops and yeast. There are also many small craft brewers around too, so if there is one of these nearby, they are worth building a relationship with (perhaps by buying lots of their beer in the first instance) then asking if they would also sell some ingredients. The advantage of going to a commercial brewer is that are likely to have the best range and freshest ingredients available because of the quantities they use, and the even greater importance to them of sourcing the best.

The first key ingredient in the process is the water, which, unfortunately, is also the only one over which most home brewers have no control. The water supply is normally fixed and cannot be changed, although there is the option of improving things with water treatments. These can soften the water, add missing elements or can just ensure consistency of supply but it is probably not essential in most home brewing, particularly when starting out. If you later decide to produce more sophisticated beers, which may require precise water characteristics, then it may be worth considering.

Just to qualify that conclusion, one of the issues with water treatments is that unless the brewer has a huge amount of experience, it is hard to pinpoint what water treatments are, or are not, contributing to the end product. There are so many other stages of the brewing process that impact upon the final outcome, the fine margins of water treatments tend to get blurred. The other issue, for the home brewer, is that the volumes of water involved mean that the quantities of water treatment being used have to be so precise that it is worth considering if it is worth the effort. The subject of treating the water supply is explained in Chapter 7.

Meanwhile, until more experience has been gained, it is probably best to focus on other ingredients and stages of the brewing process.

The next of the key ingredients is the malted barley. The dynamics of the mash are also discussed in Chapter 7 and so the focus here is on the essential properties of the malt and what it does for the beer. The malting process is very technical but in layman's terms: it essentially involves tricking the barley into the early stages of germination so it produces the various sugars it needs for the

Barley ripening in the field.
(© Darren Baker/Adobe Stock)

early stages of growth but then stopping that process and keeping the sugars stored within the grain. As part of that halting of the process, the malted barley will be hydrated, then dried and then heated. This process will also be used by a maltster to add further characteristics to the grain. So, a lighter, pale malt will be dried out and heated a lot less than a darker, chocolate malt which is 'roasted' more intensely. This impacts on the sugars present in the malt and the colour and flavour of that malt. So the more highly roasted, darker malts can have a roasted or toffee or chocolate flavour and this is directly translated to the beer (or wort) that is produced. A malt profile of pale malts will give a light colour to the end product and will not add much malt flavour and mouth feel, and so a pale ale will normally rely on the hops to add the flavour. A darker beer, like a stout, would normally rely more heavily on the malt flavour and be a much heavier beer. However, as in most things beer-related, tastes and styles are changing and there are a number of more contemporary styles of beer, such as porters, where the dark malts are used for the colour but they are not as heavily malted, with a lighter mouth feel, and are heavily hopped to give a strong hop flavour and aroma to work against the malt profile. As is becoming clear, there are the traditional beers that tend to follow a certain formula and the more contemporary beer styles that tend to mix things up a bit. Think of it as a contemporary remix of a beloved classic track, the essential elements are there but it has been twisted to give it a different feel. There is no right or wrong; like that classic track and the remix, it will come down to individual taste.

Three shades of quality malts. (© Philip Shepherd)

In summary, think of the malts as the canvas upon which the beer style is based. Play around with combinations for different colours, flavours and substance

Craft brewers checking all is in order.
(© WavebreakMediaMicro/Adobe Stock)

but always try to get the highest quality malt available. It is not especially expensive and, as the foundation of the beer, is an important starting point for the brew. Access to good and varied malts is an area that will benefit from that aforementioned relationship with a local craft brewer. Sometimes it is difficult to get hold of certain malts via the home brewing network, especially in the quantities needed, but your local neighbourhood craft brewer will probably have them and will normally not begrudge a few hundred grams.

In the mash and sparge process (Chapter 7), flavours and colour are extracted from the malt but the key element, as far as the brewing process is concerned, are those sugars that the maltster has tricked the barley into producing and then tricked again into holding within the malt. These sugars will ultimately be the food for the yeast which is converted into alcohol and CO_2, but more on that later.

Next up are the hops and these are probably the ingredient with the biggest back story and the most flexibility within the brew. Where to start with hops? There are all sorts of books about the stories behind hops and beers (Hops and Glory by Pete Brown is highly recommended), but this is a straightforward understanding/interpretation/summary:

Modern hops, in storage, after harvest.
(© Peter Maszlen/Adobe Stock)

Hops in storage after harvest, how it used to be done. (© HildaWeges/Adobe Stock)

Once upon a time, British beers were made with British malted barley and British hops. The British hop varieties tended to be very traditional and, by today's standards, quite bland. Even today, a visit to Kent or other traditional hop-growing parts of the UK normally lead to a realisation that the landscape is dotted with tall, conical building. These are oast houses and were used to dry out the hops after picking and the hops that then reached the brewer tended to be dry and low on juicy hoppiness. The upside of this drying out was that the hops lasted longer and given that a hop harvest had to last the brewers a whole year, that was the priority. As with later generations of brewers, commercial practicalities were

deemed more important than flavour, perhaps rightly in this situation.

Essentially, hops were used for their bittering qualities, hence the term 'best bitter'. This style of beer, possibly because there was not much flavour to the hops, had a fairly robust malt profile and so traditional bitters tend to be fairly dark and fairly robust. It should not be forgotten that beer was a staple of the British diet for hundreds of years because it could be safely consumed, so it really was better to drink beer – happy days! Whether this contributed to the lack of bold flavours and aromas is not clear but the volume in which beer was produced and consumed made it more of a commodity than something to be relished. This also meant that many of beers were not brewed to be particularly strong because they were being consumed throughout the day. Would the Industrial Revolution ever have happened if everyone had been drinking 6.5% hoppy IPAs? Alongside these practicalities, beer styles and strengths have been tied up with the tax and welfare philosophy of the government of the day, giving all sorts of reasons for the beers that became standard.

Alongside these dynamics, as previously mentioned, beer styles tended to be dominated by the areas in which they were brewed and the ingredients available. Clearly, water was the starting point and so beers would immediately take on the characteristics of the water in their area of origin.

Two beers bucked that trend, the first was the porter, a dark, heavily hopped beer that originated and flourished in London. Porter is an in interesting beer because its development and profile is intertwined with taxation on malts, with

A classic, rich porter.
(© Peter Kim/Adobe Stock)

A true classic, the IPA.
(© mtsaride/Adobe Stock)

darker malts being more highly taxed but producing more fermentable materials – making it still worth brewing, and also with the taxation of the beer based on alcoholic strength. The porter is a good example of a beer style developing for reasons other than consumer preference and tastes, although that was still a significant factor.

The second beer that bucked the trend was the infamous IPA, about which many legends have been created. This is not a definitive account as it is not certain that such an account exists, but this is one interpretation of the origins of the IPA. It appeared to come into its own during the 1800s and the days of the British Empire when British beer was shipped all over the world to satisfy the thirsty soldiers and the British expats now settling in foreign lands, but especially India. Initially, IPAs were not any stronger in alcohol than other beers, but they were much more heavily hopped (possibly for preservative purposes) and although they tended to be paler ales, because they were popular with drinkers in the hotter parts of the world, the beers were certainly robust. There is still an air of mystery as to what the journey did to the beer but it certainly created a whole new beer style. Stories abound concerning the journey by sea doing something to the conditioning process, or the length of the journey and the warmer climate adding to the fermentation process, but it is not completely clear what were the most significant factors. However, it certainly became very popular and, like today, adding the term IPA to the name of a beer still gave it a certain cachet.

Moving rapidly into the twentieth century, the traditional beer styles were still present but in the second half of the 1900s, things were really shaken up by the US kicking off the craft brewing phenomena and hops were a key part of that story. The temperate climates in places like Washington State meant the hops that were being grown or could be grown were far removed from the dry, bitter

The full spectrum of beer colours. (© Peter/Adobe Stock)

hops that came from the more traditional brewing areas of the world, like the UK. Perhaps this was due to a much longer growing season, which removed the need to dry and store the whole harvest once a year. But the warmer climate and the moisture also combined to produce hops that were much bolder in terms of potential for flavour and aroma, and also bitterness. The human element to this was then what the brewers did with those hops.

Three different West Coast hops. (© Philip Shepherd)

As explained in Chapter 7, the stage of the boiling of the wort at which the hops are added, changes what they contribute to that wort. If the beer style calls for a 60-minute boil, then normally the hops added at the beginning of the boil are contributing a bittering dimension. The hops incorporated towards the end of the boil, perhaps five or ten minutes from the end, are adding a flavour dimension and the hops at the end or post-boil are adding aroma. So, the abundant American hops being produced began to be used, by the brewers, more for flavouring and aroma than for bittering. This began with pale ales, because that was the dominant style of the time, but soon spread into other types – until there was a whole range of beers, based on traditional styles and recipes but with a very contemporary twist. But there was another fundamental difference between the American product and the traditional British one: back to the cask versus the keg debate.

Traditional British casks in storage. (© John Shepherd)

The more contemporary vessels, kegs, in storage.
(© John Shepherd)

Different commercial beers utilizing different hops.
(© Philip Shepherd)

As outlined in Chapter 3, the traditional cask beer differs in a number of ways from the more modern keg beer, but here the focus is on the ingredients and their impact on the beer. Suffice to say that the big, bold hoppy flavours of the American beers were well suited to keg because the greater carbonation and, normally, refrigeration enhanced those sorts of flavours. A cask enthusiast may suggest that the nature of keg requires some bold flavouring, but let's leave that discussion alone for now.

So, finally, it has come full circle and the craft beer rollercoaster has come to the UK, and while many British breweries are producing their versions of the hoppy American keg beers, especially now the can has become a popular form of packaging again, they are also producing their own cask variants. British brewers have started to develop their own versions of these beers and while many of them are moving into keg, even the more traditional cask brewers have started to look at more variety, more flavour and more aroma. From craft brewer to big multinational brewer, the IPA moniker has come back into fashion and is normally used these days to indicate more hops, more flavour and often more alcohol.

What does this mean for the home brewer? It means that there are now more choices than ever before and this gives the opportunity for experimentation; one of the great things about home brewing, with real natural ingredients. No longer confined by the pre-prepared home-brew products that try to copy favourites, if home brewers can get the ingredients then they can do what they want. Hops should probably be a focus of the ingredient 'To Do' list. It is a slightly unwinnable game to suggest that one ingredient is more important than the other, but if that was an argument that was going to be had, backing hops as that ingredient would be a sensible move.

The final ingredient is the alchemy, the magic that makes it all happen. Of course, stimulating and then extracting sugars from barley is clever and the different impacts that hops can have on the flavours of beer is intriguing and strangely logical, but it is the yeast where the magic happens.

Another quick ingredient history lesson. Yeast is a single-cell, apparently simple organism that happens to do wonderful things. It was only discovered in the 1860s by Louis Pasteur; before then it was known that fermentation took place but no one really knew how. Before brewers started adding yeast to the process, it is thought that it found its way into the beer via natural means, indeed some traditional brewers still use this method. For example, the world-famous German purity laws relating to lagers did not originally include yeast as an ingredient because they did not know it was an essential ingredient. Can there be a more appropriate definition of a magic ingredient than one which is essential to the process but of which experts were completely unaware? Once it had been

The magic of yeast.
(© Brent Hofacker/Adobe Stock)

Yeast working and fermenting in a brewery.
(© Hamik/Adobe Stock)

The single cells of yeast
(© Kateryna_Kon/Adobe Stock)

identified, those experts (as experts tend to do) hastily rewrote the purity laws to include it. Whether they also claimed that they had known about it all along but had not wanted to confuse people, is not clear.

Since yeast's discovery, hundreds of strains have been identified and for the brewer this opens up another dimension of possibilities. Essentially, in the brewing process, given the right temperature for the particular yeast, that yeast will 'consume' the variety of sugars in the wort and convert them into alcohol and CO_2 and will also add other dimensions to the flavour. (A note for any readers of a scientific background, this is not intended to be a detailed or entirely academic explanation.) The conversion into alcohol alters the density of the fluid (alcohol is less dense than water and the wort produced). It is this change in density that is measured by the hydrometer via the gravity reading. Before the yeast is added to the wort, it is denser than after the yeast has created lower-density alcohol. It is the difference between the starting density and the finished density that effectively gives the alcohol volume.

Back to the yeast varieties. Even for the small-scale, commercial craft brewer, the variety of yeasts on offer has greatly increased in recent years. The increased use of specific strains, such as New England varieties, has added another dimension to flavour and profile on top of the hops and the malts. There is not quite such an array of yeasts available to the home brewer but don't be put off experimenting

Three commercial yeasts for three different styles and tastes. (© John Shepherd)

with different yeasts, although it might be something for a little further down the road. Home brewers will almost always use dry yeasts and they tend to be slightly more generic (for example, based on the style of beer), and also tend to be slightly more forgiving in terms of conditions for use. The assumption is that this is because the home brewer is generally less able to be as precise as the larger-scale brewer, especially in terms of temperature control.

For many home brewers, the yeasts used in home brewing do a pretty remarkable job and are very consistent, so unless something goes really wrong, it is very rare for them not to work. Start simple with a generic, broad, forgiving yeast and then begin to experiment as and when confidence grows and knowledge is gained in what the other ingredients are doing to the beer.

Hopefully this chapter has given a fairly good, if basic, understanding of the ingredients but, at the risk of repeating that message, the focus is definitely on quality of ingredients above all else. Choose a supplier carefully and not only will they be able to supply quality ingredients, they can probably give some good advice too.

A typical, flexible but effective home-brew yeast.
(© Philip Shepherd)

Chapter Six
The Preparation

PREPARATION THE DAY before, or indeed on the day, is a key part of the process. It is not just that it involves the essential elements, such as cleaning, it also makes the actual brew that much easier. At certain times of the brew day, there are a few things to think about all at once, especially if new to brewing. So the more the kit is prepared, the more the process has been thought through and all the kit is to hand, the better.

Starting with the brew sheet. Some might think that a detailed brew sheet is a little over the top for home brewing but it can be as appropriate here as it is

Different ingredients for different beers.
(© Bill Doss/Adobe Stock)

at a commercial level. At a commercial level the brew sheet is probably more for consistency purposes, as it is for the home brewer, but given that experimentation can be the fun bit, the brew sheet is the record of the tweaks and fine tuning. So it is key.

There is a sample brew sheet in Appendix 1, and like everything else in this book, it is not to say that this is the only one and should be used in this format, but it is a good approach. This format works because it contains the right level of detail to guide a brewing day and to note what needs to be recorded. (Appendix 2 shows a completed brew sheet, not for recipe purposes but to show that level of detail.) There can be more or less detail in a brew sheet, depending upon how much information (and perhaps experimentation) is needed and how much prompting is required. When new to home brewing, it can be useful to also have a brewing schedule sheet (see Appendix 3) to keep things on track but, as experience grows, the brew sheet should give all the guidance that is needed.

To be useful and practical the brew sheet should be broken down into the basic historical information: beer name and date. Then a section for the key measures with expected figures and a space to record the actual figures. These figures will include expected liquor volumes at each stage (liquor is the brewing term for water; not sure why that term was chosen but let's go along with it), the wort details (wort is the brewing term for the beer/substance produced before it is fermented) for the boil and the total going into the fermenting vessel. These volumes will help with consistency of brewing and also

Taking a hydrometer reading to indicate gravity.
(© Philip Shepherd)

Checking the temperature, in order to adjust readings. (© Philip Shepherd)

Ensuring correct temperatures in the mash.
(© Philip Shepherd)

influence the volume of other ingredients, in particular hops. So, if liquid volumes are significantly higher or lower than expected, hop additions can be altered accordingly. The other key readings are around the gravity and it does not harm to measure gravity at the pre-boil stage, the post-boil stage and the bottling stage. It is the gravity readings at the post-boil and bottling stage that are most important in determining the alcoholic strength of the beer (refer to Appendix 2 for example). For total accuracy, consider taking a gravity reading of the finished beer (as it will change post-bottling for a bottle-conditioned beer) but by the time the beer is opened, drinking it rather than taking a reading from it is the more attractive option. There will be more explanation of gravity readings to follow in the appropriate sections.

The next section on the brew sheet is the details for the mash, which should include the length of the mash, the ingredients with quantities, and some more recording of temperatures and volumes. Consider how much hot liquor is going to be used in the mash stage and how much in the sparge (more on this in the next chapter) and record the temperature of the liquor before mashing. It is also important to measure the temperature of the mash at the start and then temperature at the end as these are key in ensuring that the mash does its thing and unpleasant elements and flavours are not being extracted.

The third part of the brew sheet is the boil and this will list the ingredients, the alpha acid levels of the hops, and the actual alpha acid of the specific hop batch being used. These should be adjusted, depending on volumes and acid readings to get the right bitterness (more on this later too).

Fourthly is the yeast pitch, detailing the yeast used, and the time and temperature of the wort at pitching. The final section is bottling and as well as the gravity reading, which will be recorded in the first section, always make a

Adding hops to a boiling wort. (© Philip Shepherd)

Mixing the yeast to wort in order to hydrate before adding. (© Philip Shepherd)

note of any sugar additions as this is one part of the process where the amount used will be compared to the resulting beer. This is because in order to get the optimum carbonation in the bottle for the style of beer, the correct amount of sugar needs to be added, so when the right carbonation is achieved it is important to have recorded how much sugar was used.

Given the trial and error nature of the home brewing process, it is not really possible to record too much information. The more data that is collected on the brewing process for a particular beer, the more informed are the judgements made on what worked well and what needs changing in future brews. Information is king!

Specifics regarding equipment has been covered in Chapter 4 and so the final stage of the preparation is cleaning time. Hygiene is essential at all stages of the process and, as with the gathering of information, there is no such thing as doing too much of it. The more cleaning that is done, the more confident the brewer can be that everything is sterile, giving greater reassurance that something nasty will not infect the beer.

In the brewery environment, a caustic cleaner tends to be used for the cleaning part and peracetic acid for the sterilisation. Peracetic is a great chemical for brewers because it instantly sterilises and, within reason, will evaporate without leaving any residue (assuming it has been diluted properly). However, for the home brewer, it is hard to come by, especially in appropriate quantities, and is normally only supplied on a commercial basis. So consider just the sort of chemicals that home-brew shops stock and which will still allow for both

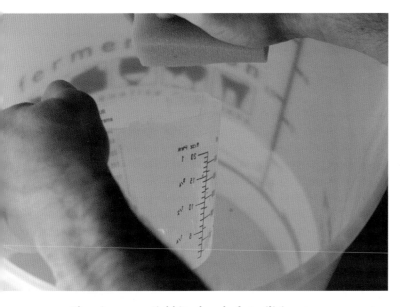

Cleaning essential kit, ahead of sterilising. (© Philip Shepherd)

Cleaning the copper/kettle, a potentially tricky job.
(© Philip Shepherd)

Cleaning the mash tun, normally a bit less tricky.
(© Philip Shepherd)

cleaning and sterilising. A lot of home brewers use sodium metabisulphate for the cleaning part and a generic non-rinse steriliser for the sterilising. Doing the cleaning on the day before brewing is usually best and the sterilising immediately before use. On the brew day try to have a fermenting bucket (clearly marked as a chemical vessel) for all sterilising as and when needed. One other thing to note is that the older and more used the equipment is, the more time should be spent on cleaning and sterilising.

If there is a need to prioritise the cleaning and sterilising process then focus on the parts of the process where the equipment is being used in a cooler environment. The mash tun and the copper (where the temperatures will be above 70 degrees Celsius) are of less importance than things like fermenting vessels and bottling equipment, which will be operating at cooler temperatures. However, having said that, cleaning is not that time-consuming and a better safe than sorry approach applies: i.e. the cleaner, the better.

Once all the equipment is clean and ready to go, it is time to start brewing. On this particular brew day, to set the virtual stopwatch running, the first stage of sterilising and getting the equipment in place begins at 7.00am; approximate timings are also detailed in Appendix 3.

Chapter Seven

The Mash and the Sparge

ON THE SAMPLE brew day, an hour is spent sterilising and getting the kit ready. The first piece of kit cleaned is the kettle and the main FV bucket. While preparing all other elements, the copper is filled and turned on.

A quick word on what is being called 'the kettle'. For most home brewers with the basic entry-level kit, the kettle has to act as both the hot liquor tank for the mash and sparge before it becomes the copper for the boil. In a normal brewery, these are two separate vessels. This dual role is not really a problem, apart from the need to clean during the brew and the need to keep an eye on the heat settings during the boil.

It is now 8.00am on the sample brew day. With the basic preparation complete it is time to begin to prepare the malt for the mash. The sample brew is going to be a fairly standard, relatively low strength pale ale, using a basic pale ale malt (Maris Otter or similar) and adding some small quantities of Carapils and Light Crystal. This just adds a slightly more complex flavour to the base of the beer and works well. If you are doing darker or heavier beers then the malt profiles become more important and you start to add greater variety. But the great thing about the malts is that there are so many different recipes and tweaks you can make. This one is a tried and trusted recipe that gives the right colour and the right balance of flavours.

Final clean of the Copper/ Kettle ahead of sterilising and use. (© Philip Shepherd)

The very basics of the malts have been referred to but, as far as the mash and the sparge are concerned, the colour and darkness of the malts used will have a close and direct impact on the colour of the beer. So a stout uses a lot of very dark malts, a pale ale a lot of pale malts, and a bitter tends to be somewhere in between. That is a very basic explanation. The purpose of the mash and the sparge is to extract as much good stuff as possible (essentially the sugars) and leave the bad stuff (by-products that come out of the malt if you overwork the mash). The malting process carried out on the barley by the maltster will ultimately

From dark to light, it's still beer, (© pavel_812/Adobe Stock)

A sample of the malt mix to be used, for the pale ale.
(© Philip Shepherd)

Weighing out the malt for the mix. (© Philip Shepherd)

determine the colours and flavours you extract but there is also a role to be played by the brewer in terms of mixing the malts when dry, to avoid overworking it later. This is pretty easy for the home brewer because the quantities are not too substantial; it is easy to just mix it all together with (clean) hands in a FV.

The first step is to weigh out your malts according to your recipe and mix them all together. If water treatments are to be used then they should be carried out

Precisely weighing out the different malts to be added.
(© Philip Shepherd)

now. Just to repeat the warning: any additions will probably require very small quantities for the home brewer, so measure these carefully.

Having weighed out the malts, cleaned the relevant kit and bought the water up to temperature, it is time to mash in. This is the point at which there needs to be some manipulating of the kettle because the target temperature for the water that is going to be added is around 70 degrees Celsius. Significantly hotter water may start to extract unwanted elements from the grain and cooler water than this is below the optimum for extracting the sugars. So to achieve the optimum 70 degrees, reduce the heat on the kettle and add some cold water if necessary.

With regard to the volume of water, it is fairly normal to use less water in the mash than in the sparge. The ratio for the sample brew is close to 2:1 (so if there are 25 litres of hot liquor to add it would be something like 9 litres in the mash and 16 litres in the sparge).

Once the quantities have been decided and recorded, add some hot liquor to

Adding the mixed malt to the mash tun.
(© Philip Shepherd)

Adding another variety of pale malt for the correct malt profile. (© Philip Shepherd)

Adding hot water/liquor to the malt at start of mash. (© Philip Shepherd)

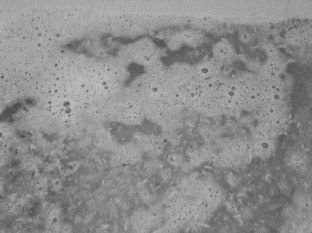

Inside the mash tun as the water/liquor soaks into the malt at the start of the mash. (© Philip Shepherd)

the base of the mash tun, then add a quarter of the malt and then a couple more litres of water and stir gently. Remember, the trick is getting all of the malt hydrated without overworking it. Having done that, add the next quarter of malt and some more water and continue until all of the malt is in and the water allocation is used. At this point the finished mash should look like a fairly thick porridge and it will thicken further as the malt absorbs the water. Then take a temperature reading of the mash, the target is somewhere between 65 and 68 degrees C. If the liquor that was added in the mash was significantly hotter than 70 degrees it will make it more difficult to achieve this mash temperature – which is why that strike temperature of the hot liquor is so important.

Record the temperature on the brew sheet, set the timer going and go and make a cup of tea. Don't wait for the mash to sit there for the whole of the allocated time, normally somewhere around an hour, because this is a good opportunity to make sure the hot liquor is at the right temperature ahead of the sparge. As with the strike temperature at the start of the mash, liquor temperature is important.

Checking the strike temperature of the mash at the outset. (© Philip Shepherd)

If it is too cool it will make the sparge less effective and if too hot may lead to extracting flavours or unwanted elements. It is essential that the water is below 75 degrees Celsius and so it's not a bad idea to play it safe and aim for about 70 degrees.

Take another temperature reading of the mash before sparging. This is largely to ensure and check consistency for future brews, because there is not much that can be done about it at this point for this brew. To give an indication: the insulation of the mash tun should mean that the mash temperature has not dropped significantly and so it will normally be fairly close to the mash temperature that was recorded at the start.

Inside the tun at the end of the mash, just before beginning to sparge.
(© Philip Shepherd)

A final temperature check before beginning the sparge.
(© Philip Shepherd)

Demonstrating the rarely seen 'colander' technique of sparging. (© Philip Shepherd)

It is now time to begin the sparge and, as well as keeping the right water temperature, the focus here is on a steady flow of water on all parts of the surface of the malt. On a small commercial brewing plant this is normally done with a rotating arm that spreads the water evenly as it rotates. A home brewer is unlikely to have such a thing and an alternative that can work on a small scale is a watering can (as this diffuses the flow of water and allows you to spread it as evenly as possible). It has been known for a home brewer to use a colander for the sparge and this would probably do a reasonable job in getting that even spread of water over the surface of the malt.

For a large mash, the key at this stage is to avoid the dreaded 'stuck' mash where flow through the mash is disrupted (usually due to compacting of the malts) and the flow from the base of the mash tun slows to a trickle. As well as making the sparge much slower it is likely to lead to an inconsistent wort profile. For the home brewer, a stuck mash is unlikely because of the volumes involved but it is best to stick to the same good practice: an even flow of water, evenly spread and aim for a thin, consistent layer of water on top of the mash. Too much water will compress the mash and too little will allow it to dry out. Both can impact the wort produced.

Set up a clean and sterilised fermenting bucket below the mash and then regulate the flow of the tap at the bottom of the tun, once again aiming for a balance, this time between a restricted trickle and it flowing out at full volume.

Start with a half closed/half open tap, then tweak it accordingly. Given that the goal is to maintain a steady layer of water on top of the malt, this suggests that the flow of water going in at the top should be as close as possible to the flow out at the bottom. For most of the mash it should be a smooth and even flow with a relatively consistent colour, although the colour of the wort coming out will slowly fade as the sparge continues; towards the end of the sparge the wort coming out of the tap will appear more and more translucent.

Once all the remainder of the hot liquor has been poured on top of the malt, the flow of wort from the bottom should continue fairly smoothly for a while but as the malt dries out the flow will slow down. This is when the more translucent colour of the wort will be apparent from the tap. Leave the wort flowing until

Demonstrating a good level of water/liquor to maintain on the surface of the mash.
(© Philip Shepherd)

The initial run-off at the start of the sparge, into the fermenting vessel.
(© Philip Shepherd)

The Mash and the Sparge **59**

The run-off becoming clearer towards the end of the sparge. (© Philip Shepherd)

it either slows to a trickle or it looks to contain a lot of floating extracts. If it becomes really cloudy, it suggests that everything desired has been extracted from the malt – but don't stop too early as the goal is to maximise the yield.

Hopefully, the process has now extracted a volume of wort close to what was being aimed for. If 25 litres of hot liquor have been used, it is reasonable to expect somewhere between 21 and 23 litres of wort, depending on how efficient the sparge has been. Make sure that the copper/kettle is empty and clean, give it a good rinse and then pour the wort from the fermenting bucket into the kettle. At this stage there is no need to worry too much about sterilising because the kettle has just had boiling water in it and the wort that has been extracted from the sparge will also be in the safe zone for hygiene.

Having mentioned temperatures and hygiene, this would be an appropriate time to talk about the temperature/cleanliness/bacteria situation. For the purposes of home brewing, the boiling point of 100 degrees Celsius will sterilise sufficiently. The next level down is pasteurisation, which is a process normally associated with packaged and non-packaged foods to eliminate pathogens. This significantly prolongs the shelf life of products like milk. Unlike boiling,

The translucent run-off at the end of the sparge.
(© Philip Shepherd)

pasteurisation does not eliminate bacterial spores and so is not as effective as sterilisation (although a second pasteurisation will be of some benefit in that it destroys spores that have germinated). If the term pasteurisation rings a bell, beyond the dairy aisle, it is because the process and research in this area was led by Louis Pasteur, he of yeast-discovery fame and largely unheralded champion of the brewing industry. Most brewers seem to use 70 degrees Celsius as a safe temperature, since the vast majority of pathogens and bacteria are not present above this level (although the spores may be).

The next level down is often called the danger zone and this is any temperature below 60 degrees Celsius, which equates to 140 degrees Fahrenheit. This explains why a brewer will see 70 degrees as a safe point: it is comfortably above 60 degrees and offers some margin for error. Below 60 degrees is where bacteria grow most rapidly and can double in as little as twenty minutes. This is important to keep in mind while moving through the brewing process because most of the actions post-boil will be done at temperatures in this danger zone.

However, this is not an immediate concern, because first it is to the kettle and the boiling of the wort, along with all the fun of the hop additions.

Louis Pasteur, a great man of science, hygiene and beer.
(© Pict Rider/Adobe Stock)

Chapter Eight
The Boil/Hopping

In very simple terms, the boil is all about adding the flavour and aroma of the hops to the wort. There are two key elements to this: one is the bitterness and the other is the more complicated flavours or notes, such as citrus, pine or floral, which have entered the vocabulary of the craft brewer. These terms tend to be more associated with contemporary beers, usually made with modern hops, which, due to their source, have different characteristics. Remember the general rule: hops added early on in the boil are for bitterness, hops added later are about more complex flavours, and hops added at the very end of the boil (or even after the boil) are about aroma.

There is more detail on types of hops and their role in the brew in Chapter 5; at this stage the recipe and beer style has been determined and the focus now is on the timings, except for taking account of the bittering quandary.

Because hops are, at their simplest and most fundamental level, bittering agents they will normally come supplied with an alpha acid reading and for the brewer this equates to the level of bitterness that could be extracted from the hops. As previously mentioned, this is of less importance with hops added at the end of the boil because you are not extracting their bitterness, but for hops used at the beginning of the boil it is vital. If the alpha acid levels of the hops are in the

Fragrant US hops full of flavour and aroma.
(© Philip Shepherd)

An adjusted measure of high alpha acid hops.

(© Philip Shepherd)

accepted/stated range of the recipe that is fine; if they are significantly higher or lower, the quantities should be adjusted accordingly: i.e. a higher than planned alpha acid means a pro-rata reduction, and a lower than expected alpha acid means a pro-rata increase in the hop quantities. Likewise, if the volume of the wort in the copper/kettle is significantly higher or lower than the recipe, bittering hop quantities should be adjusted. For example: if faced with a hop batch with a higher alpha acid and a lower volume of wort, the quantity of hops used will need to be significantly adjusted downwards.

Back to the sample brew day. Having put the wort into the copper/kettle and set the thermostat/temperature dial to boil, it is time to take a gravity reading while the wort is heating up. This particular gravity reading is not used to calculate the final gravity and alcohol content but it is the starting point for the wort. It is important to get consistency in this reading because if it is not right before the boil, it will almost certainly be incorrect post-boil and the resulting beer will not be as expected. Assuming that a consistent boil is achieved, then the gravity of the wort will normally change by the same amount during the boil (from brew to brew) and so the starting point (this reading) is the foundation upon which other readings will depend. In order to take a reading, it is important to reduce the temperature of the sample because it will either be too high for your conversion chart or, even if it is within the parameter of the conversion chart, the higher the temperature the more significant a small error in the reading will be. So the closer to the ideal reading temperature range of 25-30 degrees, the better. The easiest way to do this is to fill the sample tube and immerse the sample tube in a

Cooling the sample tube in order to get an accurate reading. (© Philip Shepherd)

jug of cold water. This sample tube can also be put in the fridge, to speed up the process. There is more detail on taking a gravity reading in the next chapter (as this is where the really important measurement takes place).

If this reading is too high then the wort can be liquored down, which means adding water to the wort to dilute it further. Not all home brewers like to do this but it is definitely a good idea for consistency. Be methodical about how much water is added; just a little bit at a time and, with experience, the brewer will get a feel for the right amount. The priority, however, is not to add too much liquor and drop it too far.

Add the liquor/water, stir it in and take another reading. Given the need to cool the sample before getting an accurate reading, this may take a bit of time and it may be necessary to turn off the kettle until you are happy with the reading. If the correct volume of water is reached but the gravity is still not right, then many brewers would be tempted to stop there. In focusing purely on hitting the gravity, adding too much liquor to the wort can result in a loss of mouth feel and taste in the final beer (it can taste literally watered down). So, at whatever point the decision is made to proceed to the boil, record the gravity reading and let the copper/kettle continue to the boil. Now is the perfect opportunity to start preparing the hops.

The recipe being used for the sample brew has a hop addition at the beginning of the boil (which in this recipe will last for sixty minutes but could be slightly

longer or shorter depending on the beer and recipe), and a second addition that goes in fifteen minutes from the end. It makes sense to adjust the hop quantities for both of these additions (based on alpha acid and wort volume) if required. The first addition would always be adjusted; the second addition, at fifteen minutes from the end, probably means it is in there just long enough for bitterness to be extracted. Also, when it comes to bittering, it is sensible to err on the side of caution because a slightly under-bittered beer is normally preferable to an over-bittered one. The third hop addition is going in five minutes from the end, and the final addition is post-boil; both of these should be adjusted based on wort volume but not based on alpha acid levels.

Weigh out the first batch of hops and be very precise on this. These initial hops are in the wort for a long time and if the quantities are not right it can significantly impact the bitterness of the final beer. Once the wort is boiling, add

Weighing out hops, following alpha acid adjustment. (© Philip Shepherd)

Stirring in the first hop addition to get a good mix.
(© Philip Shepherd)

The hops in the copper, at the start of a good rolling boil. (© Philip Shepherd)

Taking the opportunity to clean the mash tun. (© Philip Shephe

the first hop batch and give it a good stir to mix. Set the stopwatch to the next addition (the sample brew is fifteen minutes from the end of a sixty-minute boil, so the stopwatch is set to forty-five minutes).

While keeping a close eye on the kettle/copper to make sure it doesn't boil over, weigh out subsequent hop additions and clean other bits of kit (for example there is no reason a start cannot be made on the fun job of cleaning the mash tun).

Try to keep the hopping to schedule as much as possible as it does make a difference; build in a few minutes before the 'deadline' to weigh out the hops. At each stage add the hops, give the mixture a stir and set the stopwatch again. Having now done the fifteen-minute hop addition, the next is ten minutes away, at five minutes before the end of the boil.

The second hop addition added to the boiling wort. (© Philip Shepherd)

The 5 minute hop addition being added. (© Philip Shepherd)

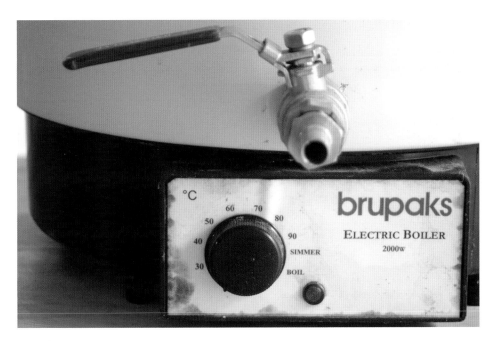

After the five-minute addition, for the sample brew, the copper/kettle is left running for those five minutes while preparing the final/post-boil hop addition (which for this recipe is the largest volume of hops). This is a hoppy beer and so requires all the aroma to be extracted from the wonderful Cascade hops. Once the copper/kettle is turned off, the final hops are added and for these post-boil hops there is no stirring in, just let them do their own thing. There is an argument for leaving the wort to cool, along with the fresh post-boil hops, for about half an hour and this is what is done here. There is no real science to this, it just seems to add something in terms of rounding off the flavour.

That's it for the boil and the hopping. Time to transfer that wort into the fermenting vessel.

The final hop addition (post-boil). (© Philip Shepherd)

Chapter Nine
The Transfer

THE TRANSFER OF the wort from the copper/kettle into the fermenting vessel (FV) is a part of the process where the difference between the commercial brewer and the home brewer is most marked. This difference in kit, and precision, continues into the fermentation process but up to this point the home brewer has largely done the same thing as the commercial craft brewer, if not, perhaps, quite as easily.

A modern brewery, both precise and shiny.
(© Ivan Kulikov/Adobe Stock)

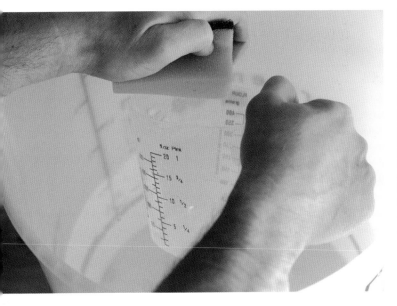

Making sure all the kit is both clean and sterilised.
(© Philip Shepherd)

Wort run-off at the beginning of the transfer.
(© Philip Shepherd)

The key parts of the transfer are to control the temperature of the wort and to keep it free from any sort of contamination. As discussed in the previous chapter, when it comes to cleanliness and hygiene dealing with liquids at more than 60 degrees Celsius is quite forgiving, but from this point, because temperatures are lower, the wort will be at more risk of contamination. So, before getting started on the transfer, be completely confident that all kit being used is clean and sterilised.

A commercial brewer will cool the fluid using a heat exchanger during the transfer, so the wort would normally be pumped from the copper, through the heat exchanger and into the FV, where it should be at the right temperature for a reading and yeast addition. The home brewer needs to transfer the hot wort into the FV bucket and then cool and take the readings.

The transfer is very straightforward for the home brewer with no need for pumps and valves; it is a matter of letting gravity do the work. Position the FV bucket under the copper, turn on the tap and decant the fluid. At the sparge the intention was a steady, not too fast, flow and at the bottling stage the focus is on avoiding getting too much air into the fluid but at this stage this is not really an issue and many brewers actually diffuse the flow to allow more air into the wort, so just pour away.

In order to maximise the yield by extracting as much of the fluid as possible, there is a balance to be struck between pouring until the bitter (quite literally) end and getting as much wort as possible without hop detritus. A home-brew copper/kettle should have some sort of basic filter or gauze to prevent the hops being sucked through the tap, so a good proportion of the wort will not take any of the hop detritus along with it. However, the very last dregs of the fluid may well contain the strongest amount of flavour (and bittering) and for this reason it is wise to play it safe and leave the very last bit of fluid in the copper/kettle.

The wort run-off towards the end of the transfer.
(© Philip Shepherd)

The cooling kit for the home brewer will normally be a cooling coil, which is fed, through a hosepipe, from a tap. The idea being that the flow of cold water through the coils (immersed in the hot wort) gradually cools down the fluid to an appropriate temperature. There are two reasons why it is vital to significantly reduce the temperature of the wort: firstly for the yeast addition (any yeast will have an operating temperature of way below the post-boil wort) and secondly to make the next gravity reading that much easier and accurate (as discussed).

The cooling coils are nowhere near as efficient as a more professional piece of

Placing the, sterilised, cooling coil going into wort.
(© Philip Shepherd)

Fixing one end of the cooling coil onto a standard domestic tap. (© Philip Shepherd)

Once connected, the cool water going in and warmed water going out at the other end. (© Philip Shepherd)

kit such as a plate heat exchanger but there are not many home brewers around who make that sort of extra investment. The standard, tap-fed coils will work but will take time, and like all water-cooling devices they will take a little longer if the water from the tap is warmer at certain times of the year – and the difference in temperature may be quite significant in the summer months.

When the wort has been cooled, take another gravity reading. This reading is what is known as the Original Gravity (the OG) from which the strength of the beer will eventually be calculated. Make this reading as accurate as possible. If the reading is still a little high then it can be liquored down again but hopefully if everything has been on target prior to the boil (including liquoring down pre-boil if required) then the post-boil gravity or OG should be fairly consistent. This is definitely an area that becomes much easier with practise. As a brewer, familiarity will grow with the beer recipes, the performance and impact of the kit and the

Liquoring down the wort to hit the correct gravity, if required. (© Philip Shepherd)

consequence of liquoring down. It may even be that the readings stated in the recipe are not realistic for the kit being used and the process being followed, so ultimately the recipe can be tweaked to gain consistency going forward.

Back to the hydrometer reading. Because of the importance of this process and the gravity at this stage of the process, this is an appropriate time to look in more detail at the taking of a reading:

1. Get sample to right temperature

The closer the temperature of the wort to the zero adjustment figure of 15 degrees Celsius, the more accurate the gravity reading will normally be. There are tables and calculators that will convert the reading if your sample is hotter or cooler than it should be, but there is always a margin for error. Having said that, because this is brewing for personal consumption, rather than for commercial reasons, it is not the end of the world if the readings are not completely as the recipe dictates; it may be that the recipe being used becomes personalised to you.

Getting the wort to the right temperature. (© Philip Shepherd)

2. Record the thermometer temperature

When happy with the temperature of the fluid then record the temperature reading.

3. Take hydrometer reading

When placing the hydrometer into the sample tube, give it a little spin with the tips of your fingers as it is released. This removes any air from the surface of the hydrometer that may impact the reading (this is because the presence of air bubbles on the hydrometer will affect the buoyancy of the device and therefore the reading). Once the hydrometer has settled and stopped bobbing in the fluid,

Checking and recording the temperature ahead of the gravity calculation.
(© Philip Shepherd)

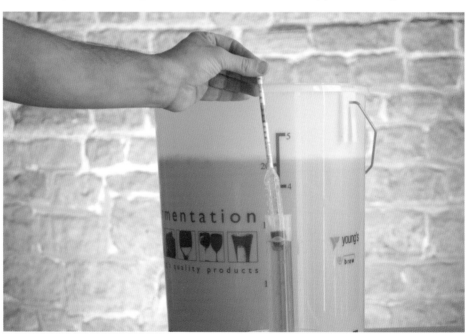

Spinning the hydrometer to remove any air on the glass surface. (© Philip Shepherd)

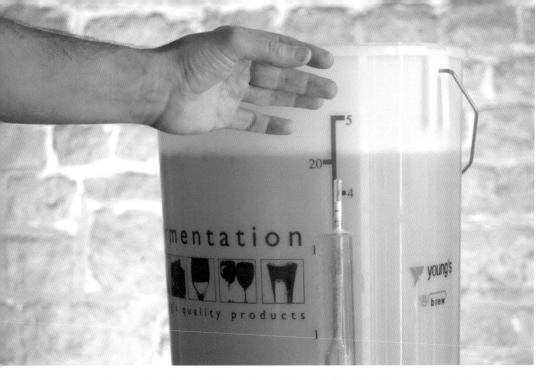

Allowing the hydrometer
to bob, then settle before
reading. (© Philip Shepherd)

take the reading from where the surface of the fluid lines up with the scale on the hydrometer.

4. Adjust as necessary

Temperature adjustment sheets are easily available online and they are a table of two columns. The first column has an ascending scale of temperatures and the second column has an adjustment figure. A couple of things to note here: the first is that if the temperature of the wort is below 15 degrees Celsius then the adjustment figure has to subtracted; if it is above 15 degrees it needs to be added. The second point is that the adjustment figures are normally written as a single digit whole number with four decimal places, for example 0.0021. The gravity readings being taken are without the decimal place and expressed around the 1000, for example 1038. But this is simple to resolve: just move the decimal point on the adjustment figure three places to the right. In the above examples if the initial reading is 1038 with the wort at 25 degrees Celsius, the adjustment figure become 0002.1 and that is what is added to the reading. The reading of 1038 is converted to 1040 (don't worry about the 0.1 at this point as it is not significant). In the sample brew, a relatively low OG of 1028 was achieved and the reading was taken at 29 degrees Celsius (an adjustment figure of 0.0032) and so the actual reading is adjusted to 1028 + 0003.2 = 1031.

That's it for the transfer at this stage. Time to get the yeast to work.

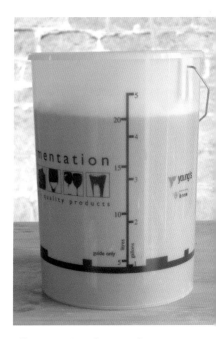

All measuring done and
adjustments made, the wort
is ready to go. (© Philip Shepherd)

Chapter Ten

The Fermentation

HAVING TRANSFERRED THE wort, reduced the temperature to the correct level and taken the all-important original gravity (OG) reading, it is time to move onto the really fascinating part of the process; the part where a sweet aromatic brown mixture is transformed into the nectar of the gods. Well, it is turned into beer anyway.

Before doing that, a quick note on the wort temperature at the yeast addition stage. When using a specific type of yeast, it is important to realise that each yeast variety is slightly different and will operate most effectively within certain bands of maximum and minimum temperature. Possibly because a home brewer's kit and approach will probably be less accurate and scientific than a commercial brewer, most home brew yeasts tend to be quite forgiving. This is great news if the brewer is happy to work with the standardised yeasts on offer, but if there is a desire to really experiment with yeast varieties (and there are some amazing ones these days), then this may identify a more urgent need to invest in some additional kit for monitoring and controlling temperature. The control of temperature at fermentation and the ongoing stability during the conditioning process, are essential for a commercial brewer, whatever the scale of operation. The fermentation will generate heat, as well as the good stuff, and so the maximum temperature during fermentation needs to be controlled. Then, once the fermentation is complete, the temperature needs to be dropped in order to both stop the yeast working and to drop it out of the beer.

Sticking with the approach of this book and, initially, keeping things simple, then select a yeast that is appropriate for the style of beer. When starting out, it makes sense to use a packaged dry yeast, rather than an active strain or culture. Many brewers will have access to a live strain that is kept 'alive' over very long periods of time and as the culture constantly 'regenerates' (apologies for the science-fiction language, compensating for the lack of pure science terminology), the yeast that is added to the wort always comes from the same source, which ensures consistency. It is a single-cell organism but it means each beer is related to the original yeast source. A packaged dry yeast will have information provided about how to add it to the wort. This advice varies from 'sprinkle on top of the wort and leave it or stir it in well' or sometimes 'hydrate the yeast before adding'. Experience suggests (and also in many home brewers' opinion) that hydrating the yeast is definitely the best option. This is not necessarily based on a great body of evidence, but just because it feels right and it always seems to work. As a home brewer: 'don't underestimate the power of what feels right 'and' if a way of doing

The yeast to be used in this particular home-brew.
(© Philip Shepherd)

things works then stick with it' and 'if it ain't broke don't fix it'. Combined, those two principles serve many home-brewers well.

The normal hydration process for the yeast is to sterilise a jug, half fill it with wort and then add the yeast to the jug (assuming that the wort temperature has already dropped down to an appropriate level). The added advantage of this approach is that if struggling to cool the wort, or it is taking a long time, this sample can be taken while the body of the wort is still too warm and, because it is a small volume, can be cooled down more quickly, meaning the yeast can be hydrated and start its work while the main body of wort is still cooling. Having added the dried yeast to the wort, give it a good old stir and then leave it for about fifteen minutes before adding the mixture to the rest of the wort. Some brewers would leave it until it is visibly doing something, i.e. building up some foam or a head on the wort, but this is another personal preference call.

Again, depending on the yeast used, effective fermentation would normally be taking place at somewhere between 15 and 20 degrees Celsius. So if it's summer

Adding the dry yeast to the wort sample. (© John Shepherd)

Yeast on sample surface. (© John Shepherd)

Adding hydrated yeast to the wort.
(© John Shepherd)

Yeast instructions and details on rear of pack.
(© John Shepherd)

then the FV can normally just be left out, if it's winter put it somewhere warm and keep an eye on it. If the yeast is working well, in just a day or so there should be visible signs of activity in the form of a heavy foam forming on the top of the wort/beer. If the ambient temperature, either actual or artificial, is warm then the fermentation will be much quicker: for example the pale ale of the sample brew as described and pictured was made in the summer and fermented out in less than two days. The packaged yeast will normally have some additional information on the labelling to confirm operating temperatures and expected performance and timescales.

Ideally, once the solution has finished fermenting or hit the appropriate gravity, then it somehow needs to be cooled to below the effective operating temperature of the yeast. This has the effect of stopping the yeast working and starting to drop it out towards the base of the beer, which makes bottling or packaging easier at the next stage. Depending on the equipment and the external environment, this may or may not be easy to achieve. A commercial craft brewer would have access to cooling equipment that allows micro-management of the temperature for optimum results. For the home brewer, just cool it as effectively as possible and don't worry too much, because the intention is to bottle condition at the packaging stage and this means dropping the yeast out at this point is not quite so significant.

Different beer styles and/or different yeasts will ferment slightly differently and this will begin to be better understood with experience. For example, a more

Fermentation stage one; full fermentation. (©John Shepherd)

Fermentation stage two; fermentation complete and yeast starting to drop. (© John Shepherd)

Fermentation stage three: yeast fully dropped. (© John Shepherd)

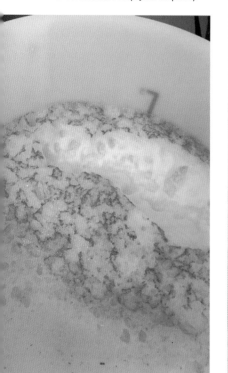

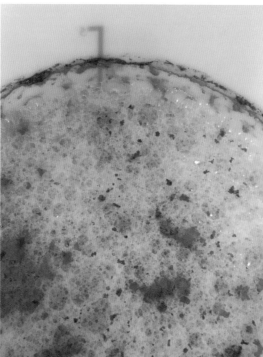

traditional yeast used for something like a best bitter tends to ferment quite ferociously and quite quickly, so normally this would be cooled down after around two days of primary fermentation, whereas some pale ales are slightly less reactive and will ferment more slowly and consistently, regardless of the conditions. The more experience the home brewer gains, the more this will become understood and it is one reason why keeping records is so important: recording timescales, temperature and gravity readings, conditions and the impact on the beer will provide a body of evidence to ensure things are on track.

As outlined previously, assuming the conditions are right, the yeast added to the wort will 'consume' the sugars in the fluid and produce two by-products: alcohol and CO_2. The alcohol will remain in the beer, changing the density of the fluid, and then the difference between this and the gravity reading after fermentation will determine the alcoholic strength of the beer. Because the humble FV bucket is effectively an open container, most of the CO_2 produced will be lost at this primary fermentation stage. This is not a problem because it will be kick-started by the yeast left in suspension and produce CO_2 when the beer is in a sealed container (in this case a capped bottle).

There is no substitute for experience in terms of knowing what to expect from the fermentation, based on beer style, ingredients and yeast, as well as the conditions, but a great thing about home brewing is that if never done before or if experimenting with something different, then it might not be possible to predict what is going to happen but it can still be observed. Keep an eye on the beer during fermentation and it will normally be apparent when it is at peak fermentation, when the yeast has done most of its work but is still doing

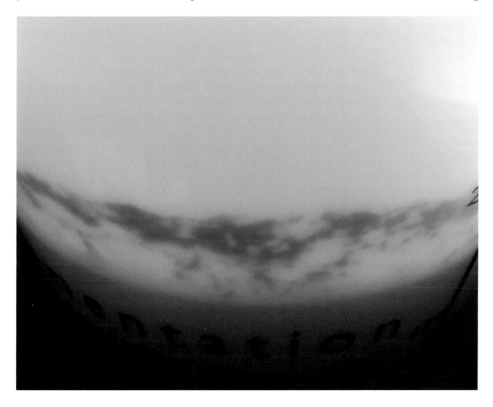

What the FV looks like after the has yeast dropped .
(© John Shepherd)

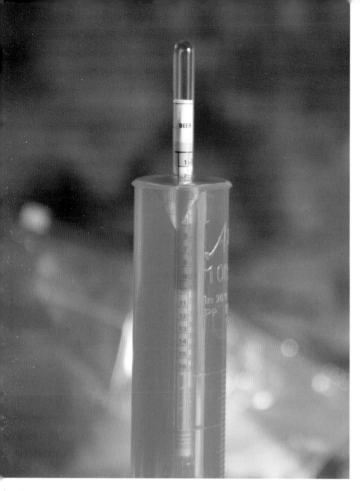

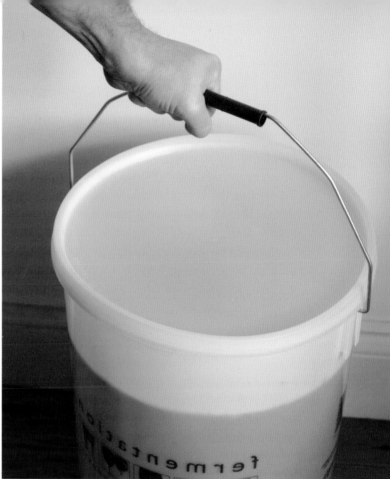

Checking the gravity ahead of making the bottling decision. (© Philip Shepherd)

Removing beer from cooling spot, ahead of bottling. (© Philip Shepherd)

something, and when it is clearly finished. Once it looks as though the yeast has done its work, take a sample and record a gravity reading and if it is close to the targeted gravity, try and get it chilled and drop the yeast as quickly as possible. If struggling to cool the wort, consider taking it off the yeast anyway and move onto packaging – although some brewers prefer to focus on the cooling and leave the beer to do its thing for the full time period. It does depend on the beer but for the pale ale being brewed as the sample, it seemed that the yeast had completed its work and it was a good time to start the packaging, which in this case is bottling.

Chapter Eleven
Packaging

IT MAY NOT be immediately obvious but the packaging is an essential part of the process. Unfortunately it can have a negative effect on the beer if not done correctly – meaning that if the packaging goes wrong it will undo all of the good work put in up to now. However, good packaging will not redeem a bad brew; if mistakes have been made in the process prior to this it will not be rescued by the packaging. So the pressure is on. Having said that, it's not really such

The bottling kit to be used for this brew. (© Philip Shepherd)

a difficult stage in the process. It does, however, require some accuracy, some cleanliness (as ever), and the recurring theme of record keeping and consistency will continue to be a factor.

Let's start with the 'three Cs' as a handy reminder of what needs to be considered throughout this stage: Cleanliness, Consistency and Conditioning. Starting with cleanliness, the 'beer' is at its most vulnerable at the point of packaging. As well as it being at a susceptible temperature, getting into the packaging normally involves multiple bits of kit and numerous opportunities for contamination to occur. So make sure everything is clean and sterilised – and that includes the person doing the packaging, and especially their hands. There is no such thing as 'too clean' at this point.

The focus of this chapter is about packaging in bottles because they are the

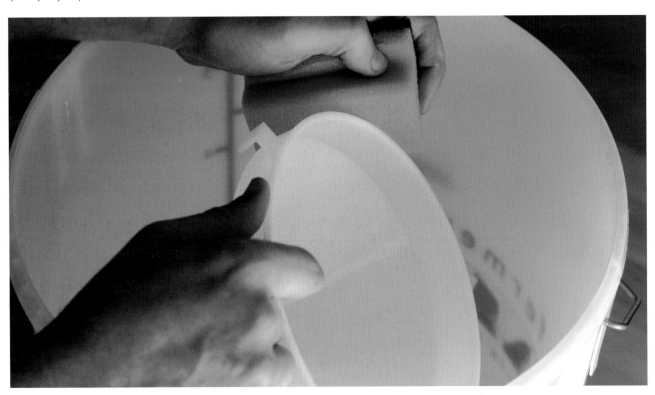

Bottles in the cleaning/sterilising FV bucket.
(© Philip Shepherd)

Rinsing the bottles to ensure completely clean of sterilising solution. (© Philip Shepherd)

Bottles placed on the cleaning rack. (© Philip Shepherd)

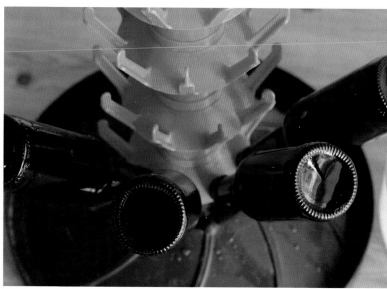

Bottles draining, to remove any excess sterilising mix. (© Philip Shepherd)

most practical, cost-effective and forgiving of packaging products and if the basics are right with bottles it is not too difficult to apply them to other forms as and when desired. So, firstly thoroughly clean and then sterilise the bottles. Reusing old bottles, either bottles previously used for home brewing or bottles that were previously full of commercial product, is absolutely fine, just make sure they are clean. It is essential that whatever the source of the bottle, the cleaning must remove all traces of yeasts, sediments and other undesirables. When sterilising bottles, most home brewers use a rack (as pictured), which both effectively drains the bottles and keeps them clean until they need to be used (ideally within half an hour or so of the cleaning).

Stacking bottles on the cleaning rack. (© Philip Shepherd)

The FV bucket to be used for bottling, with tap and bottle filler.
(© Philip Shepherd)

A basic decanting syphon ahead of use.
(© Philip Shepherd)

At the same time as the bottles, clean all the equipment, including the second FV bucket into which the beer is going to be decanted. This second FV bucket should have a tap, onto which a bottle filler can be attached.

To transfer the beer off the yeast and into another vessel, it is normal to use a syphon with the basic 'filtering' mechanism (as pictured).

If the beer has been chilled, the yeast should have settled on the bottom and these syphons can be moved around the beer, to avoid pulling through too much yeast.

Set the filter end into the beer, suck on the other end and keep the end you sucked below the level of the filter end and the process of syphoning should ensure that the beer smoothly flows into the other bucket.

Placing the syphon into the FV. (© Philip Shepherd)

Syphon in the FV ready to decant. (© Philip Shepherd)

Starting to decant into the second FV. (© Philip Shepherd) **The wort flowing into the second FV.** (© Philip Shepherd)

These syphons are also useful for allowing a good transfer of the beer into the second bucket without getting too much yeast into the beer, caused by a drop in the flow. Because the aim is to achieve bottle conditioning, it is not a problem for the odd bit of yeast to go with the flow and this can be monitored fairly easily in the tube.

As the level of the beer gets towards the bottom of the first fermenting bucket it will pick up more particles of yeast. If this starts to be constant then remove both ends of the syphon from the two buckets and go with what has been decanted.

Take a sample from the transferred beer and conduct a temperature and gravity reading on it; this will be the pre-racking measurement. It may not be the final measurement – strictly speaking one should be taken after secondary

Another gravity check ahead of bottling. (© Philip Shepherd)

Evidence that yeast has been transferred in suspension into the bottle. (© Philip Shepherd)

fermentation to measure the final gravity.

The great thing about bottle-conditioned beer is that it involves a secondary fermentation in the beer when it is in the bottle. The same thing applies in commercial brewing, if going down the cask-conditioned route, because the brewer is looking for some secondary fermentation in the cask for the same reason as the home brewer. This is one reason why brewing cask ale is slightly more straightforward than keg; filtering and strict temperature control is less important.

Although there are two by-products of fermentation, alcohol and CO_2, the main motivation for secondary fermentation is to generate the CO_2 that will add carbonation to the beer. Because this container (the bottle) is sealed, unlike the FV bucket, the beer will not lose that CO_2. Some alcohol will also be produced but nothing like the amount created in the primary fermentation. Depending on the beer style and the prior processes, just to have some yeast in the bottle and the right conditions might be enough to start secondary fermentation, but it is fairly standard to help things along with some priming sugar.

The priming sugar acts as a new source of food for the yeast that is still in suspension in the beer. In the primary fermentation, the sugars in the wort were those extracted from the malted barley in the mash tun. Most of these sugars will normally have been used up during that primary fermentation and so the yeast in the bottle will require some sugar to get things going all over again.

The amount of sugar to add will depend on the style of beer, how carbonated it should be, and how low the gravity has dropped in the primary fermentation. If the gravity has dropped below where it was expected to be, it indicates that more of the fermentable material has been used up and may need to be compensated with a higher level of sugar. If the gravity is higher than expected, it can be assumed that there is still a good amount of fermentable material and so less sugar could be needed. If everything is right where it should be, play it safe and still add a little sugar to the beer. The addition of priming sugar is a clear example of a situation that gets easier with experience and is significantly aided by keeping records. Record all gravity readings and sugar additions, and when the beer is tasted a judgement can be made on whether the carbonation is correct and how it came to be so. For the sample brew (a regular pale ale) 125g of sugar was added to 20 litres of beer; it being a hoppy pale ale there should be a good level of carbonation and so this addition is relatively large.

Measure out the required amount of sugar into a sterilised jug, add as little boiling water as is necessary to completely dissolve the sugar. Completely

The priming sugar, weighed out on the scales.
(© Philip Shepherd)

Adding the boiling water to dilute the priming sugar. (© Philip Shepherd)

Following stirring, the sugar should completely dissolve into the solution and be clear. (© Philip Shepherd)

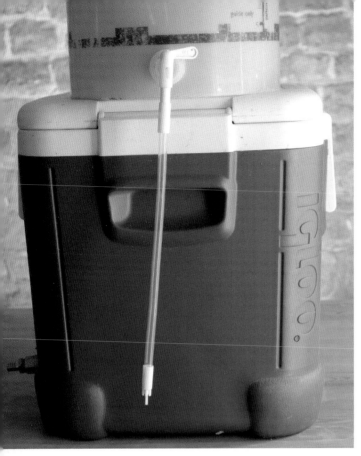

FV bucket (with tap) ready to begin bottling.
(© Philip Shepherd)

Filling the first bottle, an exciting moment for the home brewer. (© Philip Shepherd)

dissolved means the solution is clear and has no gritty sugar elements left in place. Then pour this into the FV bucket and stir well. The purpose of stirring is to get the sugar solution as evenly spread through the beer as possible and so ideally this should be done just before bottling – before the sugar starts to settle.

It is now time to start the bottling.

Raise the FV bucket into which the beer has been transferred (this should have been a bucket with a tap) and attach the very simple filling pipe (pictured) to the tap.

Then fill each bottle up to around halfway up the neck of the bottle. When six have been filled, cap the bottles. A capping machine (as pictured) has been mentioned previously and this is pretty essential and is easy to use. Place the capped beer into a box.

Once all the beer has been bottled (remember this should be done as quickly as possible so that the sugar solution remains fairly consistently in suspension), thoroughly clean all the items and tidy up.

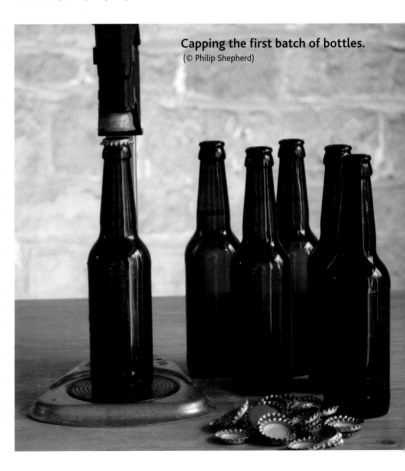

Capping the first batch of bottles.
(© Philip Shepherd)

Boxing up the filled and capped bottles. (© Philip Shepherd)

That's it. A fairly simple, but very important, stage in the process. All of the cleanliness and accuracy of things like the priming sugar now just require the right conditions in order to complete the final, but also essential, part of the brew.

Mixing up another batch of sterilising fluid. (© Philip Shepherd)

Sterilising the kit that has previously been cleaned up. (© Philip Shepherd)

Chapter Twelve
Storage

THE STORAGE OF the bottled beer is all about achieving secondary fermentation within the package. There is an expectation that there will be some yeast still in suspension in the beer, some priming sugar has been added to aid/kick-start that process and so if the bottled beer can now be stored at a temperature that is good for the yeast, then the secondary fermentation will be achieved. Assuming that the primary fermentation – in the FV bucket – worked, it is probably safe to believe that storing the bottled beer in the same place as the fermenting wort will also be effective. So, if it is summer it can be stored anywhere that has a relatively consistent temperature and if it is winter it should be stored

Different styles and different carbonation.
(© Africa Studio/Adobe Stock)

Different beers and different temperatures.
(© Ozgur Coskun/Adobe Stock)

somewhere warm, such as an airing cupboard or boiler room. Remember, the goal is to replicate the conditions and the behaviour of the yeast that was achieved in the primary fermentation.

Another quick note here on beer styles. Although to some extent this is subjective, and ultimately it is up to individual taste, but the darker, more traditional beers are normally less carbonated than the lighter, paler, hoppier contemporary styles. Recent twists on older style beers, for example heavily hopped porters that have become quite a thing, do tend to be more carbonated than traditional porters, so there is a little bit of variation here. However, a very simplistic rule of thumb still applies: old style beers with not many hops are less carbonated, contemporary well-hopped beers more carbonated. The modern beer styles are also more likely to be served chilled and although the science behind this is a little vague, chilling a beer does impact the carbonation in the beer upon drinking. Having decided what carbonation suits the beer style, and individual taste, the amount of priming sugar that is added to the beer at the bottling stage can also be adjusted.

Also, remember that the gravity of the beer at bottling stage will also impact the secondary fermentation. Most yeasts have a limit as to how low they can go as a gravity reading, so they will stop working completely or certainly slow down once they get to a certain point. Therefore, if the yeast has really dropped out and the gravity is down towards the limits of its 'comfort zone' then it will find it more difficult to drop the gravity further in the bottle, and thus potentially requires more priming sugar. Some of the maltier, heavier beers will often have more sugar from the original malted barley still in the beer at the bottling stage and so do not need as much priming. It is a balancing act.

The amount of sugar used at the bottling stage does involve a certain amount of trial and error and a lot of personal preference, but the results of the experimentation will only be revealed at the end of this secondary fermentation stage, i.e. upon opening the beer. As with lots of home brewing processes, much will depend on the ambient temperature but anywhere from a week to two weeks should be sufficient for the secondary fermentation to take place. With this pale ale test brew being followed throughout the book, the 125g of priming sugar added certainly did the job regarding the carbonation – but it was also brewed in the summer when the ambient temperatures were perfect for secondary fermentation.

At the end of this period, what happens next is up to the brewer's confidence and/or experience. If fairly confident that the secondary fermentation has completed, chill the beer in order to end fermentation and to start to drop the yeast out of the beer. If it is not chilled then the danger is that the yeast will continue to work and make the beer too carbonated. However, it does not have to be dramatically chilled; the goal is to just drop the temperature of the beer to below the effective operating temperature of the yeast: 9 or 10 degrees Celsius is normally sufficient. If not entirely confident, or as a result of being new to home brewing, that the carbonation has been achieved then open a bottle and see how it is. When popping the cap on the bottle there should be a reassuring hiss of escaping CO_2. If it is there, then it is done, if it is not then try leaving it for a few

The pale ale home-brew with an appropriate level of carbonation, for that particular style of beer. (© Philip Shepherd)

more days. Apologies for the lack of scientific rigour here, beyond a hiss, but it will give a fairly clear indication.

Don't forget that this has been packaged as a bottle-conditioned beer so, assuming that the yeast has done its thing, there will be some sediment in the bottle. Chilling the beer should drop this to the bottom but the beer will still need to be stored upright and, when poured, the last little bit left in the bottle.

That is the work done. Chill some beer, sit down, relax and enjoy the sampling. If you are still in research/experimentation mode then make some tasting notes (to influence future brews) and, if wanting to be very precise, take a final gravity reading to test the impact of the secondary fermentation. Depending on the

That opening moment and listening for the all-important hiss. (© Philip Shepherd)

The sediment that is normal in a bottle-conditioned beer, this should be left in bottle after pouring. (© Philip Shepherd)

The end product in front of the ingredients that went into creating it. (© Philip Shepherd)

result, this might influence where target gravities are set for future brews; the recipe may be tweaked to aim for slightly different gravity readings at earlier stages of the brewing process. The whole process is interconnected, so the amount of malt used will determine the maximum amount of sugar that can be extracted (and therefore how much alcohol can be produced). The efficiency of the mash and sparge will determine how much fermentable material can be extracted. The yeast used and how hard it is worked or allowed to drop will then ultimately determine strength and what takes place in this secondary fermentation.

Whilst sampling that first bottle of the first home-brewed beer, try to take a few minutes to consider whether there is anything in the end result that could be altered by doing something slightly different in the preceding process. Of course, at this point, the relief at a successful brew may be worth savouring and the logistics of how it got there could be left for another day.

Pour and enjoy, you created it. (© Philip Shepherd)

So, enjoy it, perhaps ruminate on how the tastes coming through are the result of the hard work and take pleasure in what has been achieved.

Chapter Thirteen
Next Steps

HAVING TASTED THAT first brew, assuming the results were as intended, you can now officially call yourself a home brewer. Congratulations, I hope both the experience and the end result were what you had expected. It is now time to consider where to go next.

The easiest thing to change on your next brew would be the recipe. This may just be a little tweak to what you brewed last time; perhaps you overdid it on the bittering hops but were happy with everything else or maybe the mouth feel was a little light and so you may want to boost that malt profile a little bit. Or, you may want to do something completely different and jump from a pale ale to a super-hoppy, dark and rich IPA.

It was explained, in very basic terms, at the beginning of this book what you might consider brewing in terms of beer styles, and if you want more information then there are all sorts of things to look at and recipes to browse online. In your position, consider doing something completely different for the next brew because this will help you to understand how different types of malt build a different foundation and flavour background for your beer.

As well as the malts, trying different hops with different flavours and even changing when they are added at the boil stage will impact the resulting beer. If you started with a relatively simple pale ale, as the sample brew was, why not try a hoppy porter? If you brewed a traditional best bitter, why not go for a contemporary IPA with lots of hop aroma and flavour? These are just a couple of thoughts – of course there are many different ways to go.

One slight word of caution: the more adventurous you get and the more complex your recipes, the greater the risk of potential disappointment. It is a classic case of risk and reward. But please, don't focus on this negative side of things. It takes a lot of effort and many mistakes to create a home-brew disaster through experimenting with recipes and basic ingredients (malt and hops). You are more likely to have serious disappointments in working with different yeasts and significantly different beer styles, like lagers, but other than that, be bold.

The beer styles you move onto and the recipes you use will determine the ingredients you start to play with

The basics are simple, perfection is harder.
(© chakawut/Adobe Stock)

Don't be afraid to experiment.
(© kustvideo/Adobe Stock)

but you could also consider looking at ingredients outside the usual malt, barley and hops. Flavoured beers have become much more popular, especially citrus flavours – with all manner of orange, grapefruit and other fruity elements being added. Herbs and spices are another area that home brewers have started to experiment with and wood-ageing is something that connects both craft and home brewers in terms of current trends. Similarly, you can also be clever in using ingredients to produce different styles of beer. Even some craft brewers, for example, rather than brewing a lager in the normal way (which requires different and higher-spec kit) effectively brew a pale ale-style of beer but use lager hops and malts and increase the carbonation to create a 'lager-style' product. You can do a similar thing as a home brewer, using ingredients to replicate styles that would otherwise not be possible.

A quick word here on low alcohol beers, as these are becoming increasingly popular across all sorts of beer styles. The alcohol content of the beer is driven largely by the quantity of sugar extracted from the malt, so the lower you want to drop the alcohol, for the home brewer, the more you have to drop the amount of malt used. Commercial brewers are using all sorts of other ingredients, additives and processes to reduce the alcohol content of the beer during the brew, but that is not something that is really practical for the home brewer. So consider just reducing the malts and potentially increasing other things, such as hops, which do not lead to alcohol creation. The difficult part of this process is the impact that less malt has on the body and mouth feel of the resulting beer. Achieving a really low alcohol level (0.5% seems to be the current standard) will be very tricky without quite a lot of compromise on taste and body. However, dropping the alcohol level somewhere between 1% and 2% is definitely achievable for the home brewer.

The only other word of advice on this issue is it to experiment and drop the malt volumes incrementally rather than going all out first time round. This will allow you to gradually reach a point at which the balance between body and alcohol content is achieved to your satisfaction.

Then there is the big question, the area of your home brewing domain that offers the biggest scope for change and development: the kit.

For a home brewer, you could go all the way up to what is effectively craft brewing level kit, only slightly smaller. There are 100-litre size breweries that are fairly self-contained and have a similar level of specification to a small craft brewery but are not big enough to be used commercially. This is the extravagant end of the scale; from the basic kit we have outlined throughout this book there are clearly many stops in between. As pointed out on several occasions within these pages, the basic/standard home-brew kit definitely does the job and, with a bit of imagination, can take you quite some way.

The key areas that could be potentially improved are the cooling and the bottling, as these are the parts of the process that can be really time-consuming

Low alcohol beer and the body balance.
(© Mlasaimages/Adobe Stock)

The standard home-brew equipment. (© Philip Shepherd)

or difficult and where a piece of equipment and automation can make a big difference. For example, a multi-bottling piece of kit that speeds up that process is relatively inexpensive to buy but brings a good amount of benefit. The best advice is to decide for yourself what part of the process that you would like to improve or speed up and research what is available and at what price.

One word of caution here around storage of kit. Assuming that most people have not got the space to have the kit set up somewhere permanently, always consider what you are going to do with the additional equipment when it is not being used. Home-brew equipment can be big and bulky and storing it, packing and unpacking it can get a little tiresome.

The only other area to consider regarding equipment is if you are planning some radically different beer types that would not be possible with current kit. If you were looking to produce some sort of authentic lager-style beer then you would need different equipment for the fermentation (at the very least) in order to make it genuine. This does then raise the question of investing in kit to produce something different. What becomes of it if it does not work out or if you become disinterested?

The packaging chapter only dealt with a certain type of beer – effectively bottle-conditioned – being put into a bottle. There are other options for the home brewer, with the emphasis on increased volume of packaging as much as anything

else, but these bigger containers can also offer some beer quality improvements. The 9-pint/5-litre minicasks that resemble miniature kegs and have a pull-out tap at the bottom are a great product but expensive and difficult to clean effectively enough to be re-used. The half-size casks (which at 36 pints/20 litres are just about within the reach of the home brewer) are great but also expensive. These containers, because of their size, do mean that the home brewer is getting closer to the craft brewer in terms of the packaging and because of the greater volume of beer, combined with the amount of yeast in suspension, it normally means that priming is both simpler and more consistent. If you are bottling 20 litres of beer into 40 bottles then you can get variation in the amount of priming sugar, and therefore carbonation in each. However, if the whole 20 litres goes into a half-cask then you can normally use less priming sugar, relying on the yeast to do its work without as much nudging, and with just one container consistency is much easier.

One potential way to update your kit. (© Antione/Adobe Stock)

A standard polypin/bag in a box. Good for bright beer but not for secondary fermentation. (© John Shepherd)

As ever, a word of warning with packaging: it is not really feasible to package into the polypin/bag-in-boxes that you see breweries using. Because of their lack of rigidity they are only appropriate for bright beer (beer poured after secondary fermentation with as much of the yeast removed as possible) rather than live beer (beer

The 9-pint/5-litre minicask, a great but expensive form of packaging. (© John Shepherd)

Start with pale but end up dark. (© hiddenhallow/Adobe Stock)

poured before secondary fermentation where the suspended yeast is expected to produce more CO_2 and alcohol).

Hopefully this book has given the right level of information to give you a good understanding of the brewing process, some of the science behind it and the opportunities that are now open to you.

As explained earlier, the goal of this book is to get you started, to give you the tools you need to go and experiment and learn more. Ideally, you will have enjoyed that journey, especially if you brewed for the first time alongside your progress through the book. The ultimate goal is that it has whetted your appetite and you are now raring to go and do more. One of the great benefits of home brewing as a hobby is that as well as the experience, the learning and the sense of achievement you get from doing something well, you also get something great at the end of it: your own beer, brewed to your taste and packaged in a way that suits you.

Stick with it and have many successful future brew days and tasting nights. Good luck.

Appendix 1: Sample Brew Sheet

Beer Name		
	Expected	Actual
Copper Wort Volume Pre-Boil		
FV Wort Volume		
Pre-Boil Gravity		
Post-Boil Gravity (OG)		
Gravity at Bottling		
Alcohol by Volume		

THE MASH		SCHEDULE	
Malt Types	Amounts	Grain to Liquor Ratio	
		Mash Liquor Volume	
		Sparge Liquor Volume	
		Liquor Temp at Sparge	
		Mash Temp Start	
		Mash Temp End	
Total Malt Amount		Liquor Temp at Sparge	

THE BOIL Time of Addition	Hop Variety/ Alpha Acid %	Expected to Add	Revised to Add
Yeast Type		Pitch Temperature	
Packaging Date		Priming Sugar Quantity	

Appendix 2: Sample Brew Day/Completed Brew Sheet

Beer Name	Hoppy Pale Expected	Actual
Copper Wort Volume Pre-Boil	25 litres	25 litres
FV Wort Volume	23 litres	22 litres
Pre-Boil Gravity	1035	1033
Post-Boil Gravity (OG)	1034	1032
Gravity at Bottling	1008	1009
Alcohol by Volume	3.41%	3.28%

THE MASH	70 minute mash	SCHEDULE	
Malt Types	Amounts	Mash Liquor Volume	9 ltrs
Marris Otter	3kg	Sparge Liquor Volume	16 ltrs
Carapils	200g	Liquor Temp at Sparge	70 degrees C
Light Crsytal	200g	Mash Temp Start	67 degrees C
		Mash Temp End	66 degrees C
Total Malt Amount	3.4kg	Liquor Temp at Sparge	70 degrees C

THE BOIL	65 minute boil		
Time of Addition	Hop Variety/ Alpha Acid %	Expected to Add	Revised to Add
60 mins from end of boil	EKG (6.67%)	10g	10g
15 mins from end	Cascade (7.20%)	15g	15g
5 minutes from end	Cascade (7.20%)	90g	90g
After boil	Cascade (7.20%)	40g	40g
Yeast Type	Generic Pale Ale Yeast	Pitch Temperature	19 degrees
Packaging Date	26.10.19	Priming Sugar Quantity	125g

Appendix 3: Sample Brew Schedule

Action	Time	Comments
Fill and Heat Up HLT	1 hour	
Prepare Mash Tun	30 minutes	
Add Liquor to Malt and Mash In	30 minutes	
Mash	1 hour (approx.)	
Sparge	1 hour	
Boil	1 hour (approx.)	
Transfer Wort	15 mins	
Cool Wort in FV	30 mins	
Hydrate and Pitch Yeast	15 mins	
Cleaning Up	1 hour	
Primary Fermentation	Several days	
Bottling	3 hours	
Secondary Fermentation	2 weeks	